Flintknapping

The Art of Making Stone Tools

Paul
Hellweg

IN MEMORIAM

Don E. Crabtree

(1912–1980)

During his life, Don Crabtree was unsurpassed
at skill in flintknapping. He has been
widely honored as the Dean of American Knappers, and he discovered on his own most of
the stone-working techniques described in
this book. Without his pioneering efforts,
there probably would not have been sufficient
knowledge of flintknapping to make a book
possible.

Flintknapping

the Art of

Making Stone Tools

by

Paul Hellweg

Illustrated by

MICHAEL R. SEACORD

Canyon Publishing Company

COPYRIGHT ACKNOWLEDGEMENT

Canyon Publishing Co.
8561 Eatough Avenue
Canoga Park, CA 91304

PROTECT OUR HERITAGE

AMATEUR FLINTKNAPPERS (UNLESS THEY ARE EXTREMELY CONSCIENTIOUS) CAN SERIOUSLY DISRUPT OUR ARCHAEOLOGICAL HERITAGE. BEFORE MAKING YOUR FIRST STONE TOOL, PLEASE READ CHAPTER VIII TO LEARN WHAT YOU CAN DO ABOUT THIS PROBLEM.

TABLE OF CONTENTS

ACKNOWLEDGEMENTS

I would like to express my appreciation to the following persons who helped to make this book possible:

JEFF FLENNIKEN and the late DON CRABTREE co-directed the Summer 1977 Flintknapping Field School at Washington State University. Much of what I know about making stone tools was learned that summer under the supervision of these two masters. I am therefore highly indebted to both.

DON FISHER has been more helpful than anyone else in the preparation of the manuscript. He made the set of arrowheads pictured in Chapter IV, he assisted with most of the photography, he helped with the research, and he provided general support to the entire writing project.

MILT McAULEY — my editor and publisher — provided valuable support, encouragement, and guidance from start to finish. He is responsible for the successful completion of this book.

MAXINE McAULEY did the typesetting and helped in the preparation of the book's final format.

JANET ANGEVINE assisted with the photography and provided general support.

KATHY SEACORD helped with typing, editing, and proofreading the manuscript.

JOHN H. BURTON assisted in the preparation of obsidian cores and blanks, which were subsequently utilized to make some of the artifacts pictured in this book.

STEVE TESTERMAN — with the assistance of NATHAN WARSTLER — did some important last minute photography.

LAURIE ZIMMET provided invaluable emotional support and encouragement.

And finally, a special acknowledgement for my parents, MR. & MRS. ROBERT D. HELLWEG of Bloomington, Illinois. They used much of their vacation time in California to help with the final production of the manuscript.

Paul Hellweg
Northridge, CA
1984

PHOTO #1: Examples of artifacts made by a combination of
percussion and pressure flaking include:
TOP ROW: Pendant, Charm
MIDDLE ROW: Hafted Scraper, Spearpoint, Knife Blade
BOTTOM ROW: Saw, Drill, Fishhook, Awl, Atl-atl Point
(Spearpoint is 5", all artifacts made by author.)

CHAPTER 1

INTRODUCTION

This book is about making arrowheads. It's also about making axes, knives, scrapers, mortars, and a host of other stone tools, but it's primarily about making arrowheads. The bottom line is this: you give an interested person the necessary materials and show that person how to get started, and he or she will almost invariably produce an arrowhead. I don't think this means we're all war-like or that we're preparing for a return to the stone age. Rather, I think what's being reflected is the symbolic and aesthetic appeal of the arrowpoint.

I have given quite a few demonstrations of arrowhead-making — primarily to children and college students, but also to older persons. Audiences, regardless of age, have virtually always followed the demonstrations with rapt attention. To my mind, it is an undeniable fact that many people are fascinated by arrowheads, and I would like to briefly speculate on the sources of this fascination.

As mentioned above, arrowheads seem to appeal not only to the imagination but also to our sense of aesthetics. A finely made arrowhead can most definitely be enchanting. If its proportions are carefully balanced, then it qualifies truly as a work of art. Some archaeologists even consider stone tool-making to be humankind's first art form, for they have found an abundance of stone tools in which the craftsman went beyond the mere fabricating of a functional implement. Why did early man make tools delicate and proportioned when these qualities did not enhance function? Is it unreasonable to assume that the maker was striving to achieve an ideal of perfection? And if this is not art, what is?

In addition to having artistic appeal, arrowheads seem to have symbolic and imaginative appeal. Anyone who takes the time to contemplate an arrowhead is likely to be reminded of ages long past. The beholder's mind typically fills with visions of a time when life was simple, the earth was unpolluted, humans lived in closer harmony with nature, and the struggle for survival depended upon individual strength, courage, and perseverance. I realize these are all romantic notions, but they are valid in the sense that they help explain why so many of us are fascinated with stone tools.

WHY MAKE ARROWHEADS?

The above paragraphs are mostly theoretical, and thus are not consistent with the overall tone of this book, which is primarily practical in nature. So at this point, I want to leave the theoretical behind, and examine the practical reasons people have for making arrowheads. You obviously know your reasons for wanting to make stone tools, or you wouldn't be reading this book. Still, it might be interesting to know who shares your interest, and why they do.

This discussion is largely based on a profile of those who have participated in my annual Flint-knapping Seminar at California State University, Northridge (co-taught with Don Fisher). I have found that some students take the seminar for professional reasons, but many others participate for personal reasons or for the pure enjoyment of learning a new hobby. Outright hobbyists are in the minority; however, they frequently turn out the best work. Those taking the class for professional reasons are usually either archaeologists, teachers, or both.

Archaeologists tend to be the most enthusiastic participants. It's personally rewarding for Don and and me to share their excitement as they learn to accomplish techniques known previously only in theory. Teachers, too, have been enthusiastic students of stone tool—making. A few were elementary school teachers, and they took the seminar to learn skills which could later be demonstrated to their pupils. I strongly support such educational endeavors; it's been my experience that children are eager learners when it comes to demonstrations of native Indian skills.

Finally, some of our participants have been people pursuing knowledge of wilderness survival techniques. Indeed, this is how both Don and I came to our love of stone tool-making. Originally it was just one of many "primitive" skills we tried to master; we also practiced hide-tanning, fire-starting (with a firebow, not matches), basket-weaving, pottery-making and so on. But of all these skills, we lost our hearts to flintknapping and have pursued this as our special field of expertise. Hopefully, some of you will follow a similar inclination.

BASIC TERMINOLOGY

If you're not an archaeologist, this book is likely to expose you to a whole new vocabulary. New words will be introduced and defined throughout the text, as the need arises (for the sake of convenience, a glossary has been included in Appendix I). A few terms, however, are so basic that they need to be introduced here. To begin with, this book is titled FLINTKNAPPING, and it is thus a term which should be understood from the very start. The root verb, knap, means "to break with a sharp blow." Flint is a strong yet elastic stone; it is thus the preferred material for tool-making. Flintknapping, then, is a highly descriptive term: it refers to both the raw material (flint) and the manufacturing process (breaking with sharp blows).

The breaking process is also commonly known as "flaking." Flintknapped artifacts are made by percussion flaking, pressure flaking, or by a combination of the two. Briefly, percussion flaking involves striking flakes from a rock core. This is typically the knapper's first step. Pressure flaking, on the other hand, is the process of giving an arti-fact its finished shape by pressing away small pieces of unwanted material. Depending on the material available and the knapper's skill, a wide variety of artifacts can be made by flaking. Examples in-clude spearheads, arrowpoints, knife blades, fish hooks, hide scrapers, drills, awls, charms, and so forth (refer to the accompanying photograph).

All of the above-mentioned tools are made by either percussion and/or pressure flaking. There are, however, other methods used to manufacture stone implements. Mortars, pestles, metates, manos, axes, hammers, celts, and related tools are made by a technique known as pecking and grinding. This is a different technology altogether, and it cannot be precisely referred to as flintknapping. A need thus exists for a more general term which encompasses all aspects of stone-working. Such a term is already in common use among archaeologists — they refer to stone tool-making as "lithic technology."

The word "lithic" is derived from the Greek "lithos" (stone). "Lithic" thus refers to anything involving stone. In one form or another, the word is already known to most everyone. Common examples include Stonehenge's megaliths (big stones), the paleolithic (old stone age), and the neolithic (new stone age). Lithic technology is thus not an obscure or difficult name. It includes all stone-working technologies: the knapper's percussion and pressure flaking; also, pecking, grinding, polishing, et cetera.

SAFETY

When I was but a child, my mother frequently cautioned me about the dangers of broken glass. Lit-tle did she know that I would grow up to teach classes (and eventually write a book) about a subject that involves handling lithic materials every bit as sharp as glass. As it turns out, I have already gone through several hundred bandaids in the course

of my flintknapping career. Fortunately, all my cuts
have been minor, but I have seen and heard of worse.
The danger is quite real and should not be underesti-
mated. If a stone has the right qualities for flintknapping, then ipso facto it will fracture to
extremely sharp edges. Important safety precautions
are therefore discussed wherever appropriate throughout this text. Pay particular heed to these sections; you can greatly reduce the dangers involved
in flintknapping. Above all other considerations,
you have to be safety-conscious.

GETTING STARTED

Several universities and other learning centers
offer courses in various aspects of lithic technology. Understandably, not everyone is going to have
access to such classes. This book is written, therefore, with the assumption that the reader is a novice
and will have no other source of instruction. You
should find herein all the information needed to
start making your own stone tools, and hopefully you
will find this information presented in a readily
understandable format — for that has been my goal
in writing this book.

I have attempted to organize the chapters that
follow in a logical step-by-step sequence. You
should begin by reading Chapters I — IV, and then
skip ahead to Chapter VIII, which concludes the book.
Chapter II discusses raw materials, and Chapter III
covers the basics of percussion flaking, a step that
many beginners are hesitant to undertake. But even
if someone has already provided you with a supply
of flakes for arrowhead making, you should still read
Chapter III — it gives an understanding of the mechanical principles involved in stone-working. When
you're ready to pressure flake your first arrowpoint,
you'll find everything you need to know in Chapter IV. Finally, Chapter VIII deals with ethics,
and it discusses issues of importance to all knappers, whether they be beginner or expert. The inter-
vening Chapters V, VI, and VII are more specialized

and will be of little value to the complete beginner. Read them when you are ready to expand your stone-working horizons.

Flintknapping is, of course, a skill; like any skill it requires practice to master. You can expect to make functional arrowpoints almost from the very start, but long hours of practice will be required before you're making finer specimens. Once started, however, your artistic potential as a flintknapper is virtually limitless. Hopefully, enjoyment and pleasure lie ahead.

PHOTOGRAPH ON OPPOSITE PAGE

Examples of the various minerals which can be used for arrowhead-making.

1st Row (Top): Andesite, Flint, Ignimbrite, Basalt

2nd Row: Quartzite, Jasper, Quartz, Petrified Wood

3rd Row: Rhyolite, Chalcedony, Chert, Fused Shale

4th Row: Novaculite, Opalite, Opal, Agate

5th Row (Bottom): Obsidian, Mahogany Obsidian, Porcelain, Jade (Ground)

Arrowheads made by Author

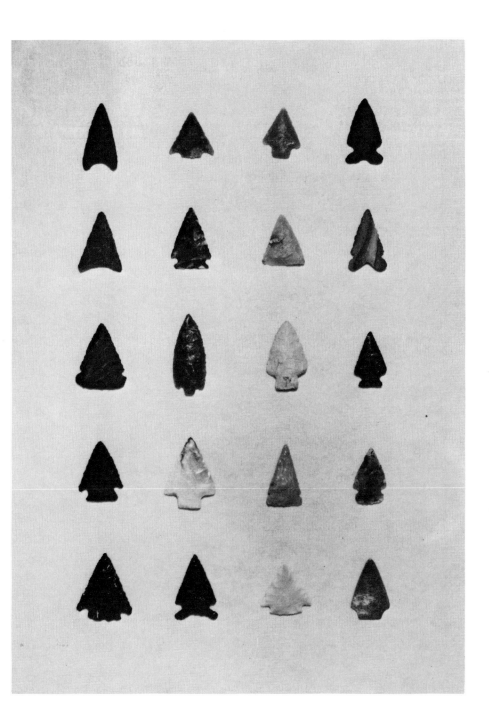

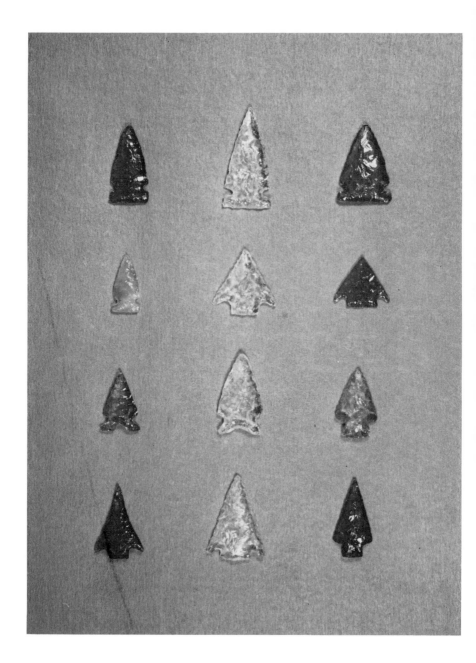

PHOTO #2: The above arrowheads are made from a variety of
          glass, including window, stained, and bottle glass
          (wine, beer, and 7-UP). Arrowheads made by Author

CHAPTER II

RAW MATERIALS

Before you can pressure flake your first arrowhead, you'll need a supply of workable stone. You can choose from nearly twenty different naturally-occurring minerals, or — if you prefer — you can get started with ordinary glass. In fact, glass is the ideal raw material, and the natural minerals are knappable only to the extent that they duplicate the characteristics of glass. In this chapter, we'll take a look at the various types of rock available and discuss their desirable glass-like properties. Also covered will be a set of guidelines for selecting your own raw material and, finally, notes on how to improve poor material through heat treatment.

TYPES OF MINERALS

The logical first step is to know which minerals have glass-like characteristics. Below is a representative list of minerals commonly utilized in the manufacture of flaked stone tools.

Agate	Novaculite
Andasite	Obsidian
Basalt	Opal
Chalcedony	Opalite
Chert	Petrified Wood
Flint	Quartz Crystal
Fused Shale	Quartzite
Ignimbrite	Rhyolite
Jasper	

Many of the above minerals closely resemble each

other, and some are difficult to tell apart. Frequently, the same material is referred to by different names. One knapper's flint, for example, may be the same stone referred to by another as chert. To avoid confusion, most knappers are in the habit of describing their stone both by type and source. Thus artifacts are described as being made of Knife River (North Dakota) Chalcedony, Flint Ridge (Ohio) Flint, and so forth.

BASIC PROPERTIES

For the most part, the above minerals are highly siliceous (as is glass). They are thus known as vitreous minerals; that is, they have the near texture and luster of glass. The reason glass is ideal for knapping is that it has no crystal structure. Glass is technically a fluid in the sense that a force applied to it will spread equally in all directions (much in the same manner that ripples spread outwards on the surface of a pond). Of importance to the knapper is the fact that it is this very ability to transfer force that makes the vitreous minerals suitable for percussion and pressure flaking.

In order to select the best material for your needs, you should have an understanding of the glass-like characteristics to seek in your raw material. Briefly, good knapping stone is:

Cryptocrystalline: the mineral's crystal structure is so small that it practically cannot be seen. In essence, the mineral behaves as if it had no crystal structure and thus transfers force in the same manner as glass.

Elastic: the mineral has the ability to return to its original state after having been depressed by the application of force. According to Crabtree, the best lithic materials are almost perfectly elastic.

Homogeneous: the material is of the same structure

throughout; in other words, it is free of any impurities or inclusions which could hamper the flaking process.

Isotropic: the material has the same properties in all directions; that is, it behaves just like a heavy liquid (sound familiar?).

In a later subsection ("Selecting Your Own Raw Material"), we'll learn how to apply the above characteristics to the process of determining whether or not a particular sample of stone is suitable for knapping.

CONCHOIDAL FRACTURE

Vitreous minerals have a property known as conchoidal fracture, and an understanding of this principle is fundamental to an understanding of the mechanical principles involved in flintknapping. It has already been seen that a force applied to vitreous minerals radiates equally in all directions; the radiating fracture lines consequently take on a cone-like appearance. The principle of conchoidal fracture is thusly named because of the resemblance between this cone fracture and a spiral conch shell.

An excellent example of conchoidal fracture is the cone formed in plate glass which has been shot with a slingshot or BB gun. When the pellet strikes the glass, the force spreads not only inwards but also outwards in ever widening circles. If the velocity of the pellet is insufficient, only a partial cone is formed. But if the pellet carries sufficient force, an intact cone will be removed from the glass (refer to accompanying drawing).

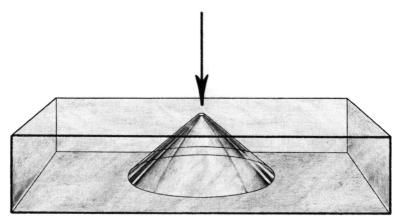

DRAWING: #1: Artist's depiction of a complete cone formed
in plate glass.

The principle of conchoidal fracture is fundamental to flintknapping for two reasons. First of
all, only lithic materials with this property will
fracture in a predictable manner. Coarser-grained
rocks do not fracture smoothly, instead they have
a tendency to crumble. Other minerals fracture only
along certain cleavage lines which cannot be controlled by the worker. It is thus only the vitreous
minerals that can be flaked according to a preconceived plan. Secondly, in accordance with the
principle of conchoidal fracture, flakes are removed
at an angle different from the direction of applied
force. The knapper must understand this principle
in order to strike flakes in the desired direction.
(For a more complete discussion of the relationship
between angle of force and angle of fracture, refer
to Chapter III.)

SELECTING YOUR OWN RAW MATERIAL

If you are interested only in pressure flaking
a few arrowheads, you can get started with ordinary
glass. Fragments of flat window glass would be best,
but pieces from any broken bottle will suffice — as
can be seen in the accompanying photograph of glass
arrowpoints. But if you desire to use authentic
materials, then you should try to obtain a supply

of obsidian. Volcanic obsidian is the natural equivalent of glass, and it is thus the ideal material for beginning knappers. It occurs throughout the American West, often in prodiguous quantities. If none is to be found nearby, then it can be obtained at most rock and gem stores (for a price, of course).

Many of the other minerals from the preceding list can also be purchased at your local rock shop. Be aware, however, that some minerals available at rock shops are very hard materials and thus will be difficult to knap. Specifically, I have had a lot of trouble working with agate, quartz crystal, and petrified wood. And a few of the others (most notably quartzite, opal, and some jaspers) are less than ideal. All in all, it really would be best to try to obtain a supply of obsidian.

For a variety of reasons, you may eventually elect to find your own field sources of raw material. Try to get someone to either guide you or supply directions, or else your first field search is likely to end in failure. When you finally do discover some likely-looking stone, you will have to use your own instincts to judge the quality of your find. We've already discussed the basic properties to look for (vitreous, homogeneous, etc.), but — understandably — these properties might be hard to interpret in a field setting. Simply stated, you're looking for material that closely resembles glass, and the following guidelines should be of help in judging the quality of prospective material:

1.   <u>Texture (luster)</u>: Carefully examine your find; generally, the smoother the texture, the easier the stone will be to work. Material of the right texture has the near luster of glass, and luster is thus an important aid in selection. Do not be deceived by the outer appearance of the stone. Most cobbles have an outer skin (properly known as the cortex) which has a texture remarkably different from the interior.

2.   <u>Sound</u>: Hold the prospective cobble in your hand and lightly tap it with a hammerstone. If the cobble gives off a dull sound, it probably has hidden cracks or fissures and is thus of suspect quality. But if

it has a sharp ring, then it most likely is of good quality.

3.   Flakability: Finally, strike a test flake. If the flake shows the correct luster, has sharp edges, is free of impurities, and did not require excessive force for removal, then you have found an excellent piece of raw material.

Under no circumstances whatsoever should Indian quarry or campsites be despoiled by an overzealous knapper looking for raw material.   The waste stone chips at an Indian site tell the archaeologist just as much as finished artifacts.   It is thus a crime, both morally and legally, to remove chips from Indian sites.   Besides, it is never necessary.   If absolutely no other material is available, remember: plain old glass works admirably.

HEAT TREATMENT

As mentioned above, obsidian is extremely easy to flake.   Many other lithic materials, however, are quite difficult to work in their natural state.   But the flaking characteristics of such stone can be improved by the proper application of heat.   To do this, the stone is buried in sand and gradually heated to temperatures in the vicinity of $260\,^{\circ}C$ $(500\,^{\circ}F)$.   Scientists are in disagreement about what happens to the stone, but it appears as if the heat drives moisture out and thereby produces microscopic fracturing.   This fracturing does not destroy the stone, rather it weakens the material to the point that it is easier to flake.

There is considerable archaeological evidence that prehistoric knappers altered their lithic raw material by heat treatment.   Heat induces color changes in most minerals, and this color change is a diagnostic aid in determining whether or not the mineral was thermally altered.   Heat treatment is not an unduly complicated process.   It can be accomplished readily in a small pit utilizing the coals of a wood fire, and was thus well within the technological capabilities of prehistoric peoples.

Heat treatment can be accomplished in an oven — but only if its temperature range is high enough. Generally speaking, the most practical way to accomplish the process is to use a pit similar to that employed in prehistoric times. You can avoid heat treating altogether by using glass, obsidian, or other material of high quality. But if your stone needs heat treatment, or if you just want to experiment with the process, then proceed as follows.

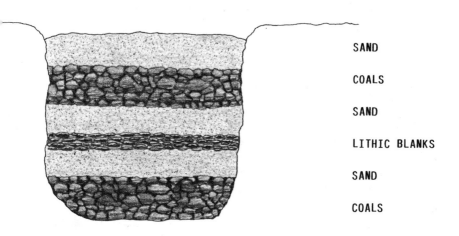

SAND

COALS

SAND

LITHIC BLANKS

SAND

COALS

DRAWING #2:   Cut-away vew of a typical heat treatment pit.

First, dig a pit approximately three feet deep by three feet wide. (If you think you'll be heat treating on more than one occasion, you can make a permanent pit by burying the bottom half of a 55-gallon drum.) Once your pit is ready, start a good blaze going in the bottom, preferably using a hard wood that will leave a bed of extremely hot coals (or simply use lots of charcoal). When you have a

hot bed of coals, cover them with a 2" — 3" layer
of sand. Now add your lithic materials to the pit,
spreading them out evenly across the sand. The
material to be heat treated should be in the form
of flakes and prepared blanks; do not add whole cobbles. Cover your lithic materials with a second
layer of sand, which should also be about 2" — 3"
thick. A second fire is started on this layer of
sand, and it too should be allowed to burn down to
a bed of hot coals. Finally, cap the entire pit with
sand, and then breathe a sigh of relief — you're done.

The key to proper heat treatment is to have the
stone gradually grow hot, then gradually cool down.
The insulating layers of sand prevent a too-rapid
transference of heat, and you control the cooling
by not uncovering the pit for a minimum of 24 hours.
Only after the pit has completely cooled are you free
to retrieve your stone. If you have carefully followed these guidelines, your material should be
thermally altered. It will now be more vitreous,
and its flaking characteristics should be noticeably
improved. You should also be able to detect changes
in luster and color.

It should be noted that the above guidelines
will not work for all stone. If done properly, the
pit will generate a temperature in the range of 260°C
to 280°C, and this is sufficient to heat treat most
minerals. However, some of the tougher and grainier
stones (such as novaculite) require temperatures up
to 500°C (932°F), and that temperature must be main-
tained for 30 — 48 hours. The only practical way
to achieve that level of heat is to leave the pit
open and to continuously stoke the top fire with
prodiguous amounts of charcoal.

If all the above sounds like too much involve-
ment for you, then you might try heat treatment in
your oven. A typical home oven will reach a temperature in the vicinity of 260°C (500°F) and thus is
capable of treating most stone (but not novaculite).
Imbed your flakes in a large pan of sand before plac-
ing them in the oven. Once again, slow heating and
slow cooling are the keys to success. Temperature

should therefore be gradually increased over a period of hours to 500°F and then left there for 10 — 12 hours before gradually being lowered. Finally, allow the pan of sand to cool thoroughly before removing your flakes. NOTE: If you are going to use a home oven, do a thorough safety check for potential fire hazards before beginning — maintaining an oven at 500° for 10 — 12 hours is going to generate a lot of heat.

Hopefully this chapter has provided sufficient information to help you procure a supply of workable stone. The next two chapters will not only tell you how to make some arrowheads from this stone, but will also discuss the remaining items you'll need to get started.

PHOTO #3: Don Fisher demonstrates correct percussion flaking
technique. Note use of goggles, gloves, and leather
pad for safety; also, ground tarp to collect flakes.

CHAPTER III

PERCUSSION FLAKING

Percussion flaking involves striking with a percussor to detach flakes or blades from a core, and it is simultaneously both the easiest and most difficult of all lithic technologies. If your main interest is making arrowheads, then all you need is to strike a few flakes. Once you have several that are good enough for arrowheads, you are finished with percussion flaking. Nothing could be simpler. In fact, if your lithic material is in the form of small chips or you are using broken glass, then you can dispense with percussion flaking altogether. At the other extreme, skilled knappers use percussion flaking to manufacture large yet delicate tools. This is flintknapping at its finest, and it cannot be done without considerable practice.

Do not confuse yourself by attempting too much too soon. For your first foray into percussion flaking, your goal should be simply learning to detach usable flakes. I have therefore limited this chapter to a discussion of fundamentals, and I have deferred advanced techniques to Chapter V. You should refer to that chapter only after you have mastered the basic skills described here.

SAFETY

Percussion flaking is potentially hazardous, and you should exercise appropriate safety precautions. Forceful and dynamic blows are required to remove large flakes. Care should therefore be taken to keep fingers and thumbs well out of the way. Also be careful of the direction flakes are struck. They sometimes fly off with considerable force, and it can be rather embarrassing to end up with one stuck in your foot (or worse yet: a bystander's foot).

Some knappers prefer to work with their hands uncovered; this allows them to better "feel" what is happening. But working with unprotected hands entails certain risks. It was while learning percussion flaking that I went through the several hundred bandaids referred to in Chapter I. The danger is not great for experienced knappers who have good control over their flaking. Beginners, however, would be well advised to wear protective leather work gloves.

Other dangers exist. A misdirected percussion blow can shatter a rock core and send fragments flying. A good pair of safety goggles is thus another necessity. In addition, you should be properly dressed. Pants of a tough fabric (such as heavy denim) obviously offer better protection than shorts or cutoffs. Finally, wear boots or heavy shoes — never work in open sandals or thongs.

In most types of percussion flaking, it is desirable to support the lithic material on the legs. A heavy leather pad is thus necessary for all knappers, beginner and expert alike. Such a pad offers protection from cuts but will not prevent bruising from a misplaced hammerstone blow. For total protection, the leather pad should be cushioned. A folded towel would suffice, but a better cushion can be made from a piece of closed-cell ensolite foam (available at backpacking and mountaineering shops).

HAMMERSTONES and BILLETS

Percussion flaking can be accomplished with a variety of percussors. Steel, wood, stone, bone, ivory, and antler have all been utilized with varying degrees of success. Most knappers, however, use either hammerstones or antler billets. Choice between these two is mostly a matter of personal preference. Some of the world's best flintknappers work exclusively with hammerstones. Others rely almost totally on billets. For the beginner, a major

consideration is availability of the different percussors: most likely it will be easier to find
hammerstones than antlers.

Choice of hammerstones depends upon the type
of lithic material to be worked. Hard flint-like
minerals require hard hammerstones. These should
be of tough granular stone and should be oval in
shape. Waterworn cobbles from streambeds are a good
source of hard hammerstones. Most knappers prefer
softer hammerstones for working obsidian, although
this material can also be worked with hard hammers.
Non-crumbly sandstone and vesicular basalt are the
best sources of softer hammerstones.

Avoid using hammerstones made of vitreous material. These will fracture with use and can project
flakes back towards the worker. They can also shatter in the hand and are a potential source of serious
cuts. In short, the vitreous minerals are raw material only and should not be used as hammerstones.

Regardless of the type of hammerstone utilized,
a good quantity should be gathered. They are subject
to breaking, and thus will need replacement. Also,
a variety of sizes are typically required. A large
percussor is needed to start work — that is, to break
up a cobble or detach large flakes. But as the flaking progresses and becomes more delicate, smaller
hammerstones are needed.

The best billets for percussion flaking come
from the antlers of moose, elk, or large deer. Only
the best quality antler should be utilized. If the
antler is old and weathered, it will be too brittle
for effective use. A billet should be made of an
antler section about 8 to 10" long, and should incor-
porate the antler base. The base end is ideal for
percussion work since it is composed of both antler
and bone, and it has little of the soft interior
found elsewhere. The billet is held and swung in
a manner similar to the use of an ordinary hammer,
and — if utilized correctly — will strike wider and
thinner flakes than those produced by hammerstones.

Availability of usable antler may be a problem.
If you have trouble locating a source, try either

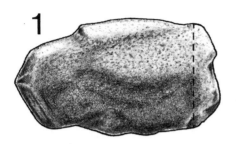

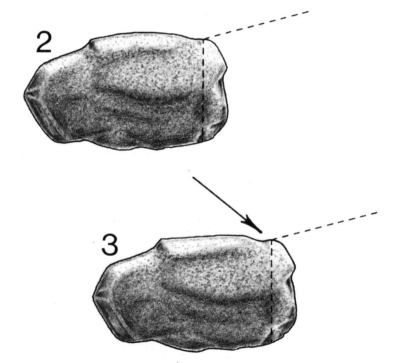

DRAWING #3: Correct striking angle is determined by applying
the principle of conchoidal fracture, as follows:
1. Envision desired flake
2. Envision that flake as part of a cone
3. Correct striking angle is now apparent

a swap-meet, taxidermy shop, or Indian curio store. If all else fails, antler preshaped into billet form may be purchased from certain archaeological supply firms. Refer to Appendix III for details.

DIRECT PERCUSSION

Percussion flaking can be accomplished in either a direct or indirect manner. Direct percussion is the basic form, and it involves striking the lithic core directly with hammerstone or billet. The beginner can use this technique to strike flakes which are subsequently worked into artifacts (flake tools). More experienced knappers use the same techniques to remove flakes selectively; thereby shaping the lithic core into a tool (core tools).

Four fundamental principles of direct percussion are described below. Using these techniques, you should be able to learn to detach good quality flakes suitable for making arrowheads. When you're ready to start making core tools or if you wish to learn about indirect percussion, then refer to Chapter V.

The four fundamentals of direct percussion are:

1. Striking Location: Size of the detached flake is determined by two factors — location of the hammerstone blow and the angle of applied force. If the hammerstone blow falls right at the edge of the lithic core, then thin flat flakes will be struck. These are the type of flakes which are suitable for working into arrowpoints or other small artifacts. But if larger flakes are desired, then strike slightly back from the edge.

2. Striking Angle: The principle of conchoidal fracture (see Chapter II) must be kept in mind when determining the best striking angle. Remember, flakes are removed in a direction different from the angle of applied force. For best results, follow these steps:

A. Visualize a desirable flake

B. Imagine that flake as a cone section

C. The correct striking angle now becomes
    readily apparent (refer to accompanying
    drawing).

The closer your striking angle is to the ideal
angle of cone fracture, the longer your resulting
flakes will be. If the striking angle is decreased
(that is, the blow comes closer to being straight-
in to the core), you run the risk of obtaining step
fractures (see next section). If the striking angle
is increased, then only short flakes will be detached.

3. Following Ridges: One rule is useful to keep
in mind when doing percussion flaking: follow
ridges. Remember, the force spreads equally in all
directions. This is true only to the extent that
there is sufficient mass to transfer the blow. In
practice, the force will spread furthest along the
ridges. In other words, you should align your hammerstone blows such that the force applied will follow an existing ridge. This can be either a natural
ridge on the core rock, or it can be the ridge left
behind by a previous flake scar. By consistently
following ridges, you will be able to strike the
longest possible flakes.

4. Platform Preparation: In order to do the best
percussion flaking, the edge of the lithic core
should have a well-defined platform (see Drawing #4).
If the natural platform is weak (slightly lipped,
etc.), it can be strengthened by light abrading.
Your hammerstone can do this task and thus serve a
dual purpose. Abrade in one direction only, OPPOSITE
to the direction flakes are to be struck.

If your core does not have a natural platform,
then you will have to prepare your own. Do this by
carefully using high angle trimming blows (see Drawing #5) to remove small pieces of material on both
sides of the desired platform. If done properly,
this will leave a well-defined and isolated platform.

34

PLATFORM ISOLATION

Excessive

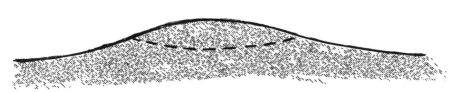

Correct

Insufficient

DRAWING #4

Top view of 3 lithic cores showing both desirable
and undesirable striking platforms.

DRAWING #5

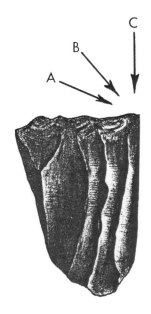

A. Proper trimming angle for platform preparation

B. Correct angle for flake detachment

C. Incorrect: too straight-in

FRACTURE ANALYSIS

The ideal flake tapers out to a feather thin edge. This is known as a feather fracture, and it is highly desired. Problems, unfortunately, can arise during percussion flaking — not all flakes will terminate in feather fractures. Two other flake termination fractures are commonly encountered: step fractures and hinge fractures (see Drawing #6). Both are difficult to work around, and they can actually ruin a lithic core.

The causes of these two undesirable fractures are outlined below. Study this section carefully because the information here is useful as a diagnostic aid. When undesirable fractures are encountered, use these guidelines to determine what went wrong. In this manner, your incidence of step and hinge fractures can be significantly reduced.

Step Fracture: A step fracture terminates a flake or blade abruptly with a right angle break. Its most frequent causes are:

1. Striking too straight into the lithic mass
2. Failure to follow ridges

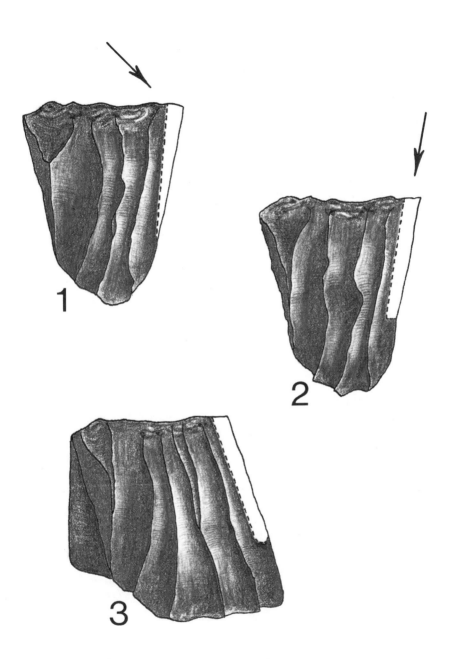

DRAWING #6: The three basic fractures are:
1. Feather
2. Step
3. Hinge

3. Poorly prepared platform
4. Insufficient blow to remove mass

Hinge Fracture: A hinge fracture terminates a flake or blade with a rounded or blunt break. Its most frequent causes are:

1. Striking on lipped edge
2. Striking on obtuse edge (edge angle greater than 90 degrees)

GETTING STARTED

Four steps are necessary before you will be ready to strike your first flake. First, you should become thoroughly familiar with the preceding sections on safety, fundamentals, and fracture analysis. Second, you will need to assemble a tool kit — gloves, goggles, leather pad, and a variety of percussors (either stone or billet). Third, you will need to find a fair supply of lithic raw material.

PHOTO #4: Pictured above are all the tools necessary to start percussion flaking: leather pad, obsidian nodule, gloves, goggles, two billets, and a variety of hammerstones.

38

(One cobble is sufficient to get started, but it won't last very long.) Finally, you'll need a place to knap. I have a friend who admits to having done percussion flaking in his bathtub. Most knappers, however, prefer an outdoor location. Your backyard should do nicely, just don't forget about the ethical considerations raised in Chapter VIII.

Percussion flaking is performed in a sitting position. I prefer to sit on a sawed-off section of log, but a chair or stool would be adequate. If you are right-handed, hold your lithic core firmly on your padded left leg. Position the core such that your intended striking platform faces to the right, as shown in the photograph at the start of this chapter. Use your right hand to hold the percussor, and deliver blows by bringing your arm down in an arc with a pronounced follow-through motion. Follow-through is very important, and you should take a few practice swings before actually attempting to strike a flake.

Do not try to smash your hammerstone or billet directly into the core. Rather, hit the striking platform with a sweep of the flat side of your per-cussor. Using the flat side allows for a slight margin of error: the blow does not have to be precise in the sense that any portion of the flat surface will do the work if it makes contact with the striking platform.

When first getting started, proceed slowly and thoughtfully. Before striking a flake, examine the lithic core. Try to imagine what the flake will look like. After the blow is struck, compare the real and imaginary flakes. If they are similar, then you probably have a good understanding of the forces involved. If they are not, don't despair — just keep practicing.

If all goes well, you should soon have a supply of usable flakes. The next chapter will discuss how to turn these flakes into serviceable arrowheads.

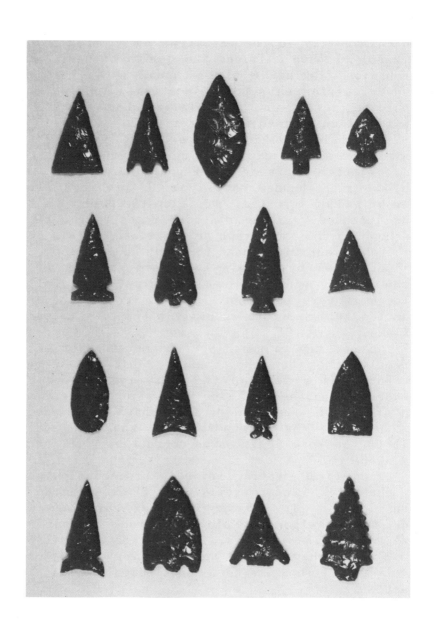

PHOTO #5: The general styles and shapes of arrowheads are shown
in this collection made by Don Fisher. These arrowheads
correspond to the drawings on pages 50 and 51.

CHAPTER IV

PRESSURE FLAKING

Pressure flaking is the process of giving an artifact its finished shape by pressing away unwanted material. A pressure tool is used to do this; it is placed on the artifact's edge and is the instrument through which force is applied. Proper use of the pressure tool allows the worker to regulate both the location and the direction of applied force. Since both of these factors are variables in percussion flaking, the pressure method offers the worker much greater overall control. It is through pressure flaking that the skilled flintknapper is able to make finished artifacts that are well-proportioned and regular in form.

PRESSURE FLAKING TOOLS

The flaking tools used by the knapper are almost as important as the choice of lithic materials. A confusingly wide variety of items will function as pressure flaking tools. The following is only a partial list of tools that have been successfully utilized by Don Crabtree: antler (deer, elk, moose, caribou), bone (limb, rib, splint), teeth (beaver, marmot, other rodents), ivory (elephant, mammoth, whale), sea shell, coconut shell, hard woods, jade, pebbles, and metal (soft iron, soft bronze, copper). Of all these, the two most suitable for the beginner are antler and copper.

American Indians commonly used pressure tools made from the tips of deer antlers (tines). Tines are strong enough to do pressure work, yet their softness allows them to grip the stone's edge. This is an important property of all pressure flakers —

especially since proper technique involves downward as well as inward pressure. Harder pressure flakers have a tendency to slip; the result is inferior workmanship plus increased danger of cuts to the workman's hands. Antlers are thus still among the best of tools. If you have trouble locating them, try either a swap-meet, taxidermy shop, or Indian curio store.

Many of today's best flintknappers prefer pressure flakers made from copper wire. Copper has the same hardness/softness characteristics as antlers, but it has the advantage of greater convenience. The copper wire is set in a wood handle which makes a better hand grip; also, the copper does not wear down as quickly as antler tines. If you're a purist, then please note: there is evidence that copper was used in prehistoric times by both the Hopewellians and the Mesoamericans.

The best copper pressure flakers are made from heavy-gauge wire. Either 2 or 4 gauge hard-drawn wire will work. Wire of this size will be approximately as thick as a 20d nail, and almost as stiff. One inch doweling makes an excellent handle for the wire. Drill a hole endwise slightly smaller than the wire, then hammer about four inches of wire into position — leaving about two inches of copper exposed. Finally, file the wire to a pencil point, and the pressure flaker is ready for use.

The copper tip will dull during use, and it will have to be continuously resharpened. This will gradually shorten the exposed wire, and eventually it will be too short for effective use. When this happens, you can revitalize the pressure flaker by simply cutting away a piece of dowel to expose a new length of wire.

Copper wire of the correct size and hardness will likely be hard to find. You will probably not be able to get it from ordinary hardware or building supply stores. It can be special ordered from electrical supply companies, but only in large quantities. Your best bet would be to check with an electrical contractor or a scrap yard that deals in used metals.

If neither copper wire or antler tines can be found, then an ordinary nail can be used. A nail can be made soft enough to use as a pressure flaker through a process known as annealing. Select a 20d or slightly larger nail, heat it till it glows red, then allow it to cool gradually (no dunking in water).

An annealed nail can be mounted in a wooden handle just as was copper wire. Drill out the dowelling as described above, and drive the nail into position. To finish the tool, simply file the exposed head to a workable point. Nails should be used as a last resort, however, since they are hard (even when annealed) and have a tendency to slip. Slipping can be avoided somewhat by keeping the working point roughened.

If you become seriously interested in making arrowheads (or other pressure flaked artifacts), you are likely to accumulate a whole set of pressure flaking tools. The tool kit of an experienced knapper is likely to include flakers of antler, copper, and perhaps steel — with several sizes of each. A variety of tools gives the worker flexibility. The larger flakers are for general work, and the smaller ones for delicate tasks (such as notching tiny arrowheads). But only one is all you need to get started.

Two other items are required to start pressure flaking: a sandstone abrader and a leather pad for protecting the hand. A small sandstone pebble (about $1\frac{1}{2}$-2") makes the best abrader, but other coarse pebbles will work if no sandstone is available. The hand pad is best made from thick, but pliable, leather. The pad should be rectangular (about 4" x 6") and needs to have a thumbhole cut in the upper lefthand corner. Finally, either a metal file or an abrasive stone is necessary to keep antler and copper properly sharpened.

If you experience difficulty assembling your tool kit, you might wish to purchase the necessary items. Everything is available commercially; for details, refer to Appendix III.

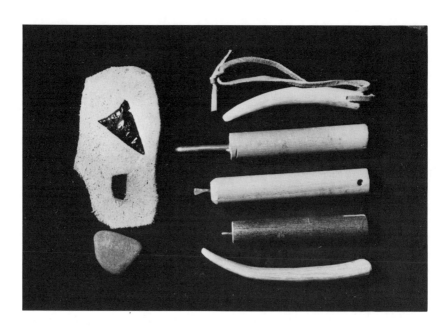

PHOTO #6: Pictured above are all the tools necessary to start pressure flaking: abrading pebble, protective hand pad, and a variety of antler and copper pressure flakers.

MAKING YOUR FIRST ARROWHEAD

A flake that is ready to be made into an artifact is technically known as a blank. The best blanks for arrowhead–making are about 1/8" — 1/4" thick (if they are thinner, there will not be sufficient mass to run flakes, and if they are thicker, you will have trouble removing the excess mass). Once you have assembled your tool kit and have a good supply of blanks, you are ready (finally) to start making stone tools. A variety of different artifacts may be made by pressure flaking. Examples include projectile points, fishhooks, drills, awls, scrapers, charms, knife blades, and so forth. But of all these, it is the arrowhead that is most commonly made. Follow the guidelines below to start making your own.

PHOTO #7: Janet Angevine demonstrates correct pressure flaking
technique. Note that this is a stable body position with
lithic blank well supported.

The original blank is likely to have extremely sharp edges. These should be ground flat in order to lessen the danger of cutting yourself and to provide a better gripping surface for the antler tine. Using the sandstone pebble, grind all edges of the blank. Resist the temptation to blow away the resulting grit; this residual material also improves the antler's grip. If you are using a piece of broken glass or other blank that has a thick edge, refer to the section on alternate flaking (under specialized techniques) for tips on how to get started.

Correct body position is important to proper pressure flaking. For best results, sit on a low stool, bench, or tree stump. The protective pad goes on your left hand, with the thumb through the hole provided. Position the working blank on your protected palm, and hold the blank securely in place

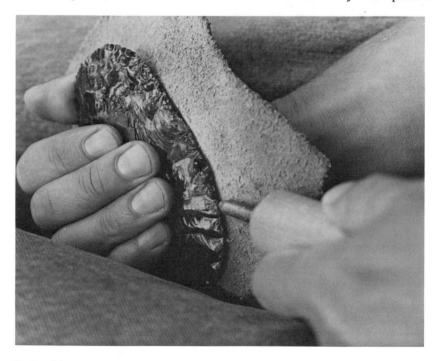

PHOTO #8: This close-up view of pressure flaking shows the proper positioning of the pressure flaking tool.

with the fingers. Work with your knees pressed together and with the left hand wedged between your
legs. This creates a stable posture with very little
danger of the blank accidentally shifting. Note:
If you are left-handed, reverse the body position
described here; that is, the leather pad goes on your
right hand, etc.

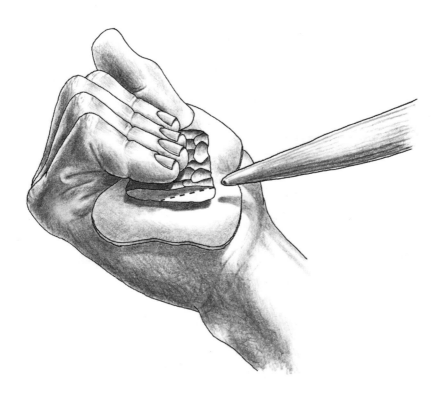

DRAWING #7: To avoid slippage while pressure flaking, the
lithic blank should be held securely as shown above.

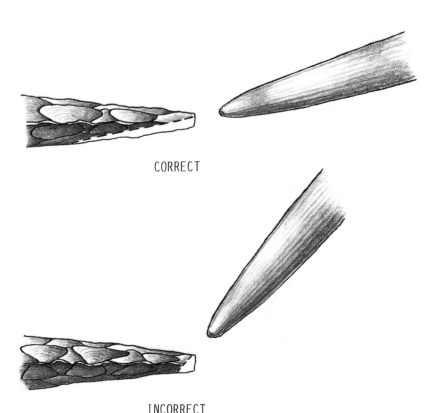

CORRECT

INCORRECT

DRAWING #8: PRESSURE FLAKING ANGLES

TOP: Correct — press nearly straight-in for long and thin flakes
BOTTOM: Incorrect — pressing at too great an angle produces only
short and stubby flakes

Carefully align the antler tine in the direction
the small pressure flake is to be removed. Flakes
are removed from the bottom of the blank; therefore,
align the antler on the bottom portion of the blank's
edge. Do not press straight into the blank, this
will succeed only in crushing the edge. The force
is best applied at a small angle from straight-in
(about 3 to 5 degrees). The closer force is applied
to this angle, the longer the resulting flake. Pressure is applied inwards, with a slight downwards
"pull" which peels the pressure flake off the bottom
of the blank. To do this properly, grip the flaking

tool securely in the right hand. Keep the wrist straight and forearm pressed close to the body, thereby eliminating unwanted shifting of the pressure flaker at the moment force is applied. And that's all there is to it. Really. Pick out some of your poorest blanks for practice. Once you've learned to run some decent pressure flakes, select a better blank and try making an arrowpoint. Do this by selectively removing material to achieve the desired shape of your arrowhead.

I've found that beginners frequently have trouble visualizing the finished shapes of their arrowheads. Refer to the photograph at the beginning of this chapter or to Drawing #9 for ideas on possible shapes. The arrowheads illustrated have been organized into general categories based on notching, base, and edge styles. They are meant as a guide only, and should not be considered a definitive classification of point styles.

When first getting started, you will probably experience the problem of having points break before they are finished. The most common causes of breakage are working with too-thin blanks and squeezing too hard with your holding hand. To put this problem in perspective, it is reasonable to expect some breakage. Try not to be too dismayed — it happens to everyone.

The hardest part of making arrowheads is getting the materials together in the first place. Once you've accomplished that, the rest will proceed rapidly. The average student is able to make decent arrowheads after an hour or less of instruction. It might take longer without instruction, but you'll probably still be surprised at how quickly you learn. When getting started, do not confuse yourself by moving on to the specialized techniques too rapidly.

SPECIALIZED TECHNIQUES

This section will discuss four new techniques: platform preparation, alternate flaking, notching,

GENERAL POINT STYLES

TRIANGULAR

BARBED

STEMMED

SHOULDERED

LEAF

DOVE-TAILED

NOTCHING STYLES

SIDE-NOTCH

BASE-NOTCH

CORNER NOTCH

NOTCHLESS

DRAWING #9a: PROJECTILE POINT STYLES

BASE STYLES

CONVEX BASE   CONCAVE BASE   NOTCHED BASE   STRAIGHT BASE

EDGE STYLES

STRAIGHT EDGE   CONVEX EDGE   CONCAVE EDGE   SERRATED EDGE

DRAWING #9b: PROJECTILE POINT STYLES

and ridge alignment. Using these techniques, you can progress from the simple fabricating of crude points to the manufacture of finely shaped master-pieces.

Platform Preparation: In order to run long pressure flakes, the antler must be positioned on a well-defined platform. Use the sandstone abrading pebble to prepare this platform. Holding the blank firmly, roughly abrade in ONE DIRECTION only. Then turn the blank over and run your pressure flakes in the OPPOSITE DIRECTION. This rough abrading in the opposite direction establishes the clearly defined platform which is necessary for long pressure flakes (see drawing).

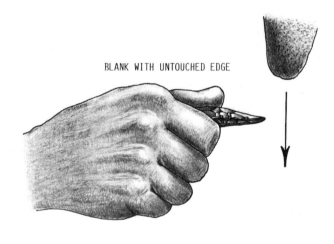

BLANK WITH UNTOUCHED EDGE

BLANK WITH PREPARED PLATFORM

DRAWING #10. To improve pressure flaking results, prepare a platform for the antler tine by abrading in a direction OPPOSITE to the intended direction of flaking.

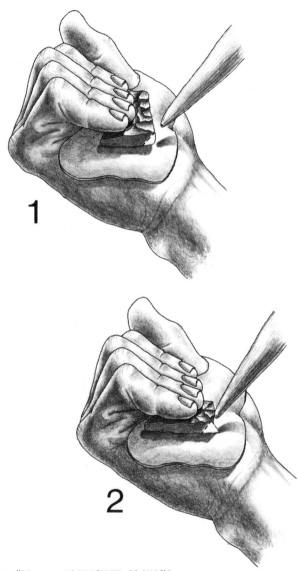

DRAWING #11.   ALTERNATE FLAKING
1. Hold flaking tool at a high angle (about 45°) and press
    off a short stubby flake from one corner.
2. Turn blank over and use previous flake scar as platform
    to remove second short stubby flake (also at 45° angle).
    Continue back and forth until entire thick edge is
    removed.

Alternate Flaking: Normal pressure flaking is next to impossible on blanks with thick square edges. These troublesome edges are best removed by alternate flaking; that is, by removing pressure flakes from alternate sides. Start at one corner and remove a short stubby flake by changing the angle of the antler tine to about 45 degrees. Then flip the blank over and remove a similar short stubby flake from the opposite side. For this second flake, do not position the tine on the blank's original edge. Instead, start the second flake from the new edge created by removing the first flake. Continue in this manner until the entire thick edge is removed. Each time, flip the blank over and start from the newly exposed edge left by the previous effort (refer to drawing). Once the entire edge is removed, then the rest of the blank may be worked by standard pressure flaking techniques.

Notching: Many aboriginal points were made without notches, and thus it is not necessary to notch modern-made ones. Notching, however, is quite common; sooner or later you'll need to learn the technique. It is not difficult and you're already familiar with the basic principle — it's just another form of alternate flaking.

A small pressure flaker is helpful. But if you have only one, then file it to a sharp point. To start the notch, run a short stubby pressure flake at the desired point. This is done by shifting the pressure tool from its normally low angle (3-5 degrees) to a high angle (about 45 degrees). Then flip the arrowhead over and run a short flake from the opposite side. Use the scar left by the first flake as the platform for the second. Continue alternate flaking in this manner until the notch is cut to its desired depth. But be careful here. Notching is a delicate task, and many are the fine arrowheads broken by carelessness.

Ridge Alignment: The chapter on percussion flaking discussed how the force of a blow travels furthest along existing ridges. The same is equally true of pressure flaking. If the antler tine is

54

positioned such that force is applied in the direction of a ridge, then longer pressure flakes can be achieved. The skilled artisan thus utilizes the ridge left behind by the preceding pressure flake. You can do this too by carefully positioning the antler tine for each effort. Whatever the width of the previous flake, move the tine about half that distance for the next. This then aligns the center of the new flake over the ridge left behind by the previous flake. By continuing in this manner, each pressure flake will have a ridge to follow.

Master flintknappers like Flenniken and Crabtree take the ridge alignment technique one step further: they prepare their own ridges. Examine a pressure flake scar, and you'll notice it looks somewhat like an upside down teardrop. The ridges left by the flake scar do not run straight to the blank's edge; instead they curve towards each other. If a ridge were to run straight to the edge, then it would do a better job of transferring the force when pressure is applied for the next flake. This is the point where the master knapper creates his own ridge. He does this by altering the existing ridge so that it in fact does run straight to the margin.

This is a difficult technique to master and is not recommended for beginners. But if you want to give it a try, then proceed as follows. Visualize in your mind what the existing ridge would look like if it ran straight instead of curving. Notice that the difference between a curving ridge and a straight ridge is a tiny triangle of lithic material. Very, very carefully position the pressure tool atop this tiny triangle and snap it off. If you successfully remove this triangle of unwanted material, then you will have succeeded in straightening the ridge. It is now ready to transfer your next pressure force with optimum efficiency.

It is not necessary to master the specialized techniques to start making decent arrowpoints. But if you would like to make larger or more delicate points, expect to spend a lot of time practicing. With sufficient practice you could soon be turning out your own works of art.

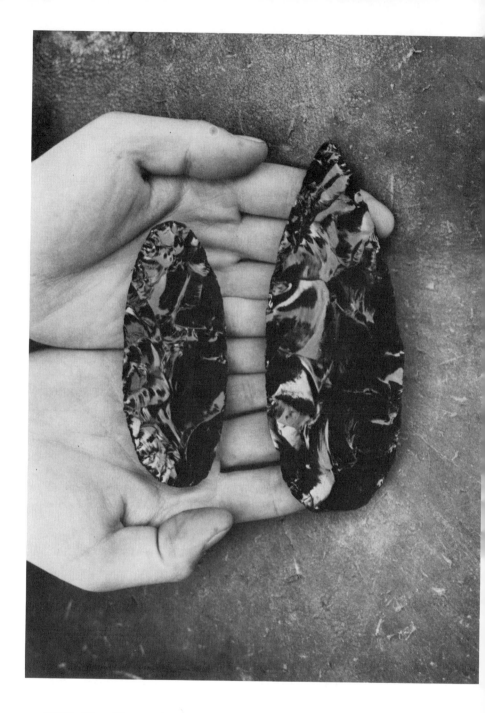

PHOTO #9: Pictured above are two examples of bifaces made by
the author.

CHAPTER V

ADVANCED TECHNIQUES

By now you should have a fair understanding of percussion and pressure flaking, and you should be making some reasonably decent arrowheads. Many knappers are satisfied at this point, and do not further pursue the study of flintknapping. But if you desire to learn more, then this chapter is for you. Though this chapter does not include a look at all possible flintknapping technologies, you will find enough here to keep you occupied for quite some time. Specifically, the following subjects are covered: Indirect Percussion, Percussion Blades, Biface Reduction, Fluting, and Burin Manufacture.

I have tried to give sufficient information to get you started on these advanced techniques; however, to be honest, it may not be possible to master these techniques without the assistance of an experienced knapper. If you have no one to turn to for help, then be prepared for a lot of "trial and error" flintknapping. Try not to get discouraged. With time, patience, and considerable practice, you should be able to overcome the difficulties of working alone.

INDIRECT PERCUSSION

You have already learned about the basic form of percussion flaking (direct percussion), but to round out your skills, you might like to try indirect percussion flaking. Indirect percussion involves the use of an intermediate tool to transfer the force of the percussor. Various materials will serve as the intermediate tool, but an antler punch is undeniably the best. A good-sized antler tine is required, preferably one of elk. The punch will be stronger if its tip is blunt. In use, the punch is positioned at the edge of a prepared platform and then struck with either a hammerstone or heavy billet.

The great advantage of indirect percussion is that the punch is positioned before the blow is struck. This controls both striking location and striking angle. The punch technique is thus much more accurate and reliable than direct percussion. Also, the punch detaches straighter and more uniform flakes (particularly if the core is rested on a wood anvil). Because of these advantages, indirect percussion is used in two aspects of lithic technology: manufacturing blades and working large bifaces.

DRAWING #12. The ideal core for blade production should have a flat top and well-defined ridges, as seen above.

Indirect percussion does have one notable draw-back. Generally, two persons are required: one to hold the core, and one to hold both the punch and deliver the blow. And unless workers are extremely careful, the punch technique poses increased danger to their hands. It may be possible for a skilled knapper to overcome these problems. The core can be held between the feet, or it can be held in an impro-vised vice. But for most knappers, indirect percus-sion is a two person technique.

PERCUSSION BLADES

A blade is a specialized flake that is more than twice as long as it is wide. Blades are highly use-ful flakes and are frequently used as tools with little or no modification. They also make excellent blanks for fabricating knives, dart points, and other artifacts. Blades are occasionally struck during the normal course of percussion flaking. They are so de-sirable, however, that several technologies exist just for their manufacture.

Both direct and indirect percussion can be used to manufacture blades. Direct percussion is easier, but it yields short and curved blades. Indirect per-cussion, on the other hand, yields excellent blades that are long, thin, and straight. The only drawback is that indirect percussion is difficult to execute (see above).

Blades are struck from specially prepared cores, which are roughly cone-like in appearance. The flat bottom of the cone is the striking platform of the blade core. Before blades can be struck, the core itself must be prepared. It needs to have a broad flat surface for its striking platform. Many nodules are found with naturally occurring flat spots. If you have some, you're in luck. If not, then you will have to prepare your own by splitting the nodule in half. To accomplish this, rest the nodule on an an-vil stone, and deal it a hefty blow with a good sized hammerstone. Once you have a core with a flat sur-face, percussion flake it into an approximate cone shape.

59

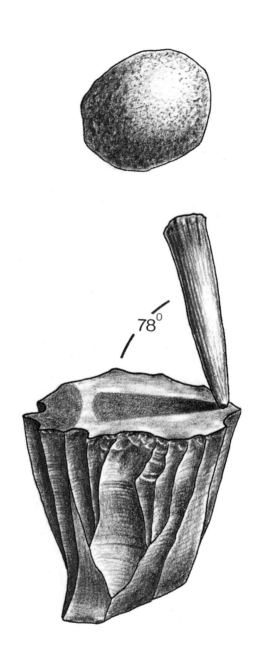

DRAWING #13. INDIRECT PERCUSSION
   Position antler punch at an angle of approximately 78^0 to the
lithic core, as shown above.

You are now ready to strike blades. The blades must follow ridges, otherwise they will spread out and terminate short. Use a naturally occurring ridge (or a ridge left from core preparation) to strike the first blade. Then use the ridge left by the first blade to strike the next, and so forth. The core is likely to need constant attention. Should the striking platform become lipped, it will need to be abraded flat. Also, turn the core as blades are struck in order to utilize the core's entire circumference. As successive blades are struck, the core will become increasingly cone-like in appearance and will be gradually reduced in size. Continue striking blades until the core is no longer serviceable.

BIFACE REDUCTION

When aboriginal knappers mined lithic raw materials, they usually would not bother to haul cobbles and nodules back to their villages. Instead, they typically percussion-flaked nodules down to portable blanks before leaving the quarry site. These percussion flaked blanks are known today as bifaces. Technically, a biface is any artifact which has been flaked on both sides; but in common usage, the term refers only to percussion flaked blanks.

Refer to the picture at the start of this chapter to see two examples of finished bifaces. Now try to visualize something similar inside your own obsidian or flint. Bifaces are made by direct percussion in accordance with the principles outlined in Chapter III. The only difference is that much greater skill is required. When a cobble is reduced down to a biface, flakes are removed selectively according to a preconceived plan. In order to do this, you must have sufficient experience to be able to control both the size and the direction of your flakes.

Producing a biface is a refined skill, and it may not be possible to learn from a book. But if you would like to give it a try, your first step should be to thoroughly review direct percussion basics.

The fundamentals (striking location, striking angle, following ridges, platform preparation) are all very important to biface reduction, and they must be kept constantly in mind. Everything else in Chapter III is important too: you'll be encountering step and hinge fractures, you'll need to remember correct body position and so forth. Finally, don't forget the safety requirements — they are particularly applicable here.

As you get started, you should support your lithic core directly on your padded leg — just as outlined in Chapter III. But as the biface begins to reach its general shape, you will probably want to hold it directly in your left hand. This can be a little dangerous, so don't forget to wear protective gloves. Also, it is important to grip the biface firmly; the pressure exerted by your fingers will hold flakes in position and thus prevent their flying back into your palm. And in order to achieve all-around stability, your hand holding the biface should still be supported (on your padded leg).

Proceed slowly and thoughtfully, and — as described in Chapter III — try to visualize each flake before it is detached. The angle of cone fracture remains unchanged, but this angle may be harder to visualize on a biface than on a rock core. A drawing of biface striking angles is therefore included here — hopefully this will be of help in determining the correct striking angle.

The real challenge of creating a biface is to make it flat and thin. Thinning flakes are best struck from the side margins. If you try to thin from the ends, you will probably only succeed in making a shorter biface; also, you will run increased risk of breakage through end shock (see below). When thinning from the side margin, correct striking location and striking platform are very important. Refer to Drawing #4 (Chapter III) and Drawing #15 (here) for help in visualizing these variables. Note in Drawing #15 that a properly prepared striking platform involves slightly beveling the biface's side margin. Use high angle trimming blows to isolate and bevel your striking platform.

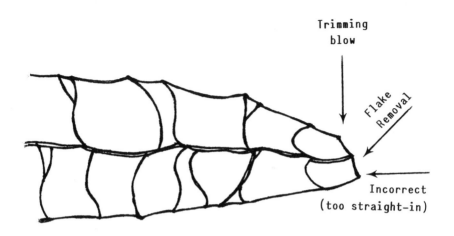

Trimming
blow

Flake
Removal

Incorrect
(too straight-in)

DRAWING #14:   Biface striking angles

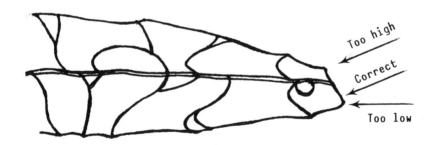

Too high

Correct

Too low

DRAWING #15:   Biface striking location

As you become proficient in biface reduction, you will likely start to experience two new types of fracture: end shock and perverse fracture. Both of these will ruin a biface, but you shouldn't be discouraged. If anything, you should be delighted. I say this because it takes a considerable amount of skill to thin a biface to the point that it can be broken in half. Your first end shock or perverse fracture is thus a sure sign that you are well on your way towards mastering biface reduction. Of

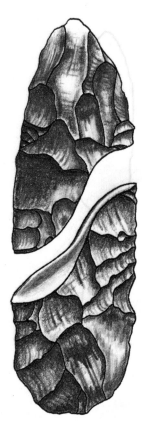

PERVERSE FRACTURE   END SHOCK

DRAWING #16: Types of fractures frequently encountered during bifacial reduction.

course, you don't want to break all your bifaces, so refer to the information below to learn the cause and prevention of these fractures.

1. <u>End Shock:</u> a fracture which runs straight and which has a slightly lipped edge. It is caused by the application of excessive force to an end of the biface. To prevent, either do not strike from the end, or — if you must strike an end — support the opposite end on a hard wood anvil.

2. <u>Perverse Fracture:</u> a spiral or twisting fracture which typically does not run straight. It is caused by striking a side margin with too much force or by attempting to remove too large a flake (again, from a side margin). To prevent, use less force and/or a better platform.

To summarize this section on biface reduction: the manufacture of bifaces is a skill which will take considerable practice to master. But if you persevere, your rewards will be many. A thin and delicate biface is truly a work of art, and you can justifiably take pride in your efforts. More importantly, bifaces make superb blanks for pressure flaking spear heads, knife blades, and related large artifacts. In short, biface reduction is a lot of work, but it is a skill you will need to master if you are to progress beyond the mere making of arrowheads.

FLUTING

Fluted points bear large longitudinal flake scars, typically on both sides. They are important historically because they represent some of the earliest point types (Clovis, Folsom, Sandia, etc.) to be found in this country. Long before the introduction of the bow and arrow, spears with fluted points were utilized in the hunting of mammoth, bison, and other large animals. Though fluting technology is very old (it dates back well over 10,000 years), it is a sophisticated technology and it requires great

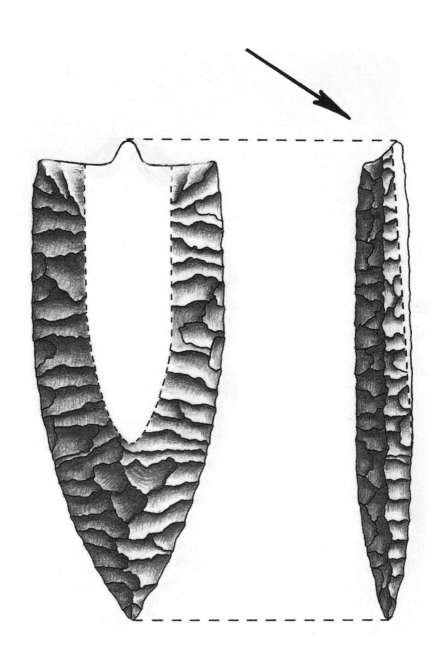

DRAWING #17: To run a long and thin flute, prepare a pronounced
nipple—like striking platform, as shown above.

skill to master. Fluting is thus not for the beginning knapper — it has been included here primarily because of its historical significance.

If you would like to experiment with fluting, you will first need to make a good supply of bifacially prepared blanks. These can be as short as two inches for Folsom points, but should be longer for Clovis points (such as the one shown in Drawing #17). To prepare a blank for fluting, pressure flake a pronounced nipple on one side only. This nipple is your striking platform. The flute spall can be removed by either indirect percussion or direct freehand percussion. For indirect percussion, have a brave friend hold the blank upright while you position the antler punch and deliver the blow. Direct freehand percussion is a little simpler: use a small hammerstone or billet to strike directly on the nipple (keeping in mind the correct angle of cone fracture). Regardless of the technique you choose, you should do two things: 1) Support the blank on a hard wood anvil to reduce the danger of end shock, and 2) Use gloves and a leather pad to protect the hand which holds the blank (the danger of serious cuts is very real).

When (if?) you are able to successfully flute one side, turn the blank over and prepare a new nipple on the opposite side. Once both sides are fluted, pressure flake the point to its desired shape. Finally, to finish the point to prehistoric authenticity, the side edges near the base should be ground flat (so they won't cut the hafting cords). Now frame the point and display it prominently — your efforts are worthy of recognition.

BURIN MANUFACTURE

A burin is a chisel-like implement used to carve wood and bone. They are intriguing little tools that can be put to a variety of uses. If you have artistic inclinations and would like to carve decorations on the handles of your stone-age tools, then you'll

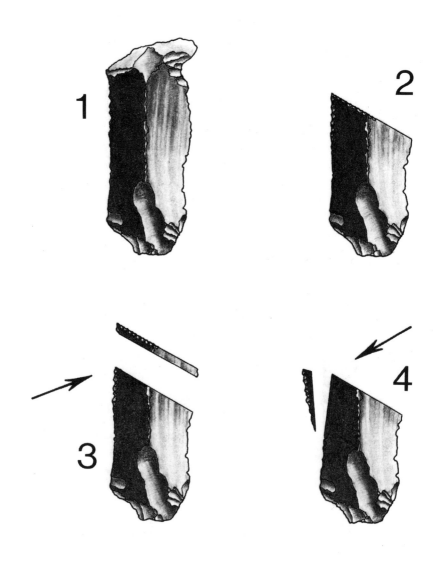

DRAWING #18: The four stages of burin manufacture are:
1. Select a serviceable blade
2. Truncate the blade
3. Remove 1st burin spall
4. Remove 2nd burin spall

need a burin. Also, a burin is useful in the manufacture of some tools, such as the "backed-blade"
knife described in Chapter VII. To make a burin,
follow these four steps (refer to Drawing #18):

1. Obtain a percussion blade (discussed earlier in
    this chapter).

2. Using either percussion or pressure flaking,
    truncate the burin at an oblique angle.

3. Remove first burin spall. This is best done by
    tapping the blade against a hammerstone.

4. Remove second burin spall. This too can be done
    by tapping the blade against a hammerstone.

If the above steps are done properly, the junc-
tion of the two spall scars will leave a sharp-edged
chisel point. This manufacturing process really is
pretty simple — the only hard part is obtaining a
suitable blade in the first place.

CONCLUSION

As I mentioned earlier, most of the techniques
described in this chapter are rather difficult. But
they have been mastered by contemporary knappers, and
they can be mastered by you. All it takes is a lot
of practice (and maybe a few bandaids).

PHOTO #10: The author demonstrates correct technique for pecking
a stone axe into shape.

CHAPTER VI
PECKING AND GRINDING

In this chapter, we'll be taking a look at a totally different aspect of lithic technology. It's called "pecked and ground stone technology," and it is not at all related to percussion or pressure flaking – except for the obvious fact that all are methods for working stone. Briefly, pecking and grinding is the technique used to manufacture hammers, axes, celts, mortars, pestles, metates, manos, food mullers, and related stone tools. Since most people show greater interest in hammers and axes than in implements of food preparation, this chapter will focus primarily on the manufacture of the former.

As has been seen, the technique for making hammers and axes is known as "pecked and ground stone technology." This appears to be an appropriate name because it identifies the two distinctive manufacturing stages involved. The first stage is "pecking" the artifact into rough shape through repeated blows with a hammerstone. Each blow removes minute quantities of material through crushing or crumbling effect, and the artifact is thus gradually shaped. The second manufacturing stage consists of grinding the artifact into finished form. Grinding is the wearing away of material by abrasion, and is the technique used to put the sharp edge on an axe, celt, or related chopping tool.

By now, it probably has become obvious that "primitive" tools are not really primitive. This is particularly true of stone axes and hammers. A properly made stone axe, for example, will readily cut down a fair sized tree. A good working axe takes considerable time to manufacture, thirty to forty hours not being unreasonable. On the other hand, a decent hammer can be made in an hour or two. The reason for such a pronounced difference in manufacturing time is that axes need to be made from harder materials than that used for hammers. A look at raw material would thus seem to be the appropriate place to begin.

PHOTO #11: Axe on the left is made of fine-grained basalt and took approximately 40 hours to manufacture; hammer on right is made of a coarse-grained stream cobble and took less than an hour to make.

BLANK SELECTION

The quality of a finished hammer or axe does not depend primarily on manufacturing techniques. Rather, it depends on the degree of hardness of the stone from which the implement is made. A coarse stone such as granite can be quickly shaped into a useful hammer, food muller, or related tool. But granite is not suitable for use as an axe. A granitic axe could be made in an hour or two, but it will not hold an edge and would likely wear out in less time than it took to make. Genuinely efficient chopping tools must be made from rock much harder than granite.

Basalt and andasite are two of the best materials to utilize for quality axes. Tools made from one of these can be resharpened over and over and will last seemingly forever.

Selection of a proper stone to use as the raw material, or blank, is thus a matter of importance since it determines the quality of the finished implement. Blank selection also relates directly to manufacturing time. When planning a new axe–making project, it is not unreasonable to spend several hours looking for the "perfect" blank. The rationale is simple. Five hours spent looking for a good blank is time well spent if it saves ten hours in the manufacturing process. The closer the blank resembles the proposed artifact in size and shape, the less material that will have to be removed in the shaping process. And having less material to remove obviously reduces manufacturing time.

The ideal axe blank would be a piece of fine-grained, extremely hard rock. These will have a smooth texture and will be comparatively heavy for their size. They must be free of cracks, and thus must be inspected closely. Also, a good blank is homogeneous, that is, of similar consistency throughout. Any change of texture reflects a potential weak spot, and nonhomogeneous blanks should be bypassed. Remember, coarser–grained blanks are suitable for hammers, but not for axes.

HAMMERSTONES

Of equal importance to the selection of a proper blank is the choosing of a good hammerstone. The pecking hammerstone should be of a rock harder than the stone to be worked, and it too should be homogeneous and free of cracks. Any good hard stone will suffice; however, a siliceous stone of flint, chert, quartzite, or related material would be superior. (Siliceous refers to silicon bearing rock — in other words, the same type of stone from which arrowheads are made.) The working edge of an ordinary hammerstone will become blunt with use. In contrast, tiny pieces will flake off a siliceous hammerstone. Instead of dulling, a flint or quartzite hammerstone will continuously resharpen itself during use. In short, any hard rock will work, but a siliceous hammerstone will greatly speed up the pecking process.

PECKING

Once blank and hammerstones have been selected, the first step in manufacture is to use the hammerstone to peck or pound the blank into the approximate shape of the proposed artifact. The process is simple enough, but some disagreement exists as to the proper techniques. The rationale behind my methods can best be explained by reviewing the process through which I came to know them.

I originally learned that the rock being shaped by pecking should not be supported on a hard surface. Instead, I was taught to hold the rock loosely in my hand in order to lessen the danger of its cracking under continuous pounding. But at the WSU field school, Jeff Flenniken explained that hand-holding was inefficient. The supporting hand "gives" with each hammerstone blow, thus the blow's force is dissipated and a good portion of the craftsman's effort is wasted. Clearly Jeff was right, and this put me in a bit of a quandry. Experience indicated that if the axe blank is supported on an anvil rock, then it did indeed have a tendency to shatter or crack. Yet having been exposed to Jeff's ideas, I was no longer content to waste time and effort working without support for the piece being worked.

My solution to the support problem is far from profound, but it is practical. The tree stump which I formerly sat on while working has shifted roles. It is now my anvil, and it has proven to be ideal. It offers sufficient support to eliminate wasted effort. More importantly, it is soft enough to give some cushioning and thereby significantly reduces the danger of breaking the rock being shaped. I have done a great deal of work since the field school, and

I remain convinced that supporting the blank on a stump, log, or other wood is by far the most efficient method of pecking.

Another area of disagreement which needs to be addressed is whether or not water is beneficial to the pecking process. In theory, at least, it should be. Presumably water would fill the pores of the stone being worked and through a mini-hydraulic effect would transfer the force of each blow over a wider area. However, I remain unconvinced. I attempted an experiment under carefully controlled conditions: weighing twenty specimens to the nearest 0.01 gram before and after use, recording pecking time, and so forth. My results were inconclusive. Variation from stone to stone (even under identical test conditions) was too great to mean anything. My own opinion, which admittedly is not backed up by incontestable evidence, is that water is of no use for working fine-grained basalt and andasite, and of only limited value for coarser-grained rocks. And that limited benefit is offset by the water's tendency to hold waste material in place and thus obscure the working surface. I find that I get the best results by precisely aiming my hammerstone blows at "high" spots. This I cannot do with the working surface obscured, thus I prefer to work without water. But until more accurate experimental results can be obtained, the use of water appears to be a matter of personal choice.

If making a hammer, only a hafting groove need be pecked out. This can be accomplished in as little as a half hour under ideal conditions. For a hammerhead, the hafting groove should be placed at the center of balance. For axes, on the other hand, the groove should be positioned well aft — at the point where the center of gravity is likely to be after the blade end is thinned and sharpened. Pecking an axehead will take considerably longer than the simple grooving of a hammerhead. This is due in part to the harder nature of a good axe blank. Also, the shaping of an axe is more involved since the blade should also be pecked into its approximate shape prior to grinding.

Rather than trying to imitate a jack-hammer, you should make your hammerstone blows deliberate and methodical. If a steady rhythm is developed, more work can be accomplished in the long run than can be achieved through brief energetic spurts of activity. Each blow should be moderately hard — light taps are unproductive; heavy pounding risks breaking the stone being shaped. Continue pecking until the hafting groove is cut to desired depth, and the entire tool has been worked into its approximate shape. If making a hammerhead, it is now complete and ready for hafting (see Chapter VII). But if the artifact is intended as a chopping or cutting tool, one more stage in manufacture is required — grinding the blade to a sharp edge.

GRINDING

Grinding is best accomplished on an abrasive rock such as sandstone or decomposing granite. Smoother rock can be used for grinding if sand is added as an abrasive. The axe is pressed firmly down, and rubbed back and forth methodically. The grinding slab should be rinsed periodically to cleanse off accumulating waste material. The grinding process is tedious, but no special skill is required until the final shape is almost reached. At this point, grinding becomes more delicate and the artisan must be attentive. As the blade nears completion, the final shaping should be accomplished in one direction only — away from the body. If final abrading is done in both directions, then small particles are apt to be broken or pulled off during the backward stroke. Such rough spots cannot be accepted on the cutting edge of a finished axe because they serve as potential footholds for larger breaks when the axe is put to use.

Rough spots will sometimes occur on the blade, even if precautions are taken. When this happens, the edge must be "backed off" beyond the trouble spots. Hold the axe straight down on the grinding slab and abrade until the edge is round and smooth.

PHOTO #12: The axe blank is first roughly shaped by pecking

PHOTO #13: Once the rough shape of the axe head is prepared
through pecking, final shape is achieved by grinding.
Notice the groove worn in this sandstone slab from
many hours use.

PHOTO #14: The final step in preparing the axe head is sharpening the blade. A small piece of smooth sandstone is rubbed over the cutting edge at an angle of about 20 degrees (this is done in a manner quite similar to sharpening a steel knife).

PHOTO #15: The completed axe ready for hafting. This one is made from basalt and required about 35 hours to manufacture.

Then repeat the final shaping process, being extra careful this time.

Another feature to be careful about is the angle of the cutting blade. The first celt (a specialized form of axe) I ever made had a very sharp cutting edge, but the blade tapered too thickly to that edge. When I put the celt to use, I was dismayed to find it grossly inefficient. I've since found that thinner blades make for vastly superior tools (refer to accompanying photograph).

PHOTO #15a: The celt on left has a sharp cutting edge, but is not an effective chopping tool because the blade is too thick. Celt on right has a thinner blade and has proven to be an efficient tool.

Before leaving this section on grinding, I would like to throw in a parenthetical note: it's possible to use the grinding technique to make arrowheads, charms, and other small artifacts. Grinding works particularly well on some stones which are not otherwise suitable for arrowhead-making. Specifically, ground stone arrowheads can be made from jade, slate, and turquoise. Also, the grinding technique can be used to make artifacts from shell and bone. To grind an arrowhead, select a small flattish piece of raw material. No skill is required; simply abrade the blank back and forth until the desired shape is obtained. You can even notch your ground stone arrowheads: if your grinding slab has a tough sharp edge, use that edge to grind notches.

SHARPENING

Once the blade is ground as sharp as possible on the grinding slab, it is time to hone the edge to cutting perfection. This is done in much the same manner as sharpening a knife. In fact, a wetstone may be used if available. If not, select a smooth sandstone pebble and rub the axe bit edgewise with a circular motion. During sharpening, the wetstone or sandstone pebble should be held at about a twenty degree angle to the axe blade (the same angle used to sharpen a steel knife). Continue until the finished edge is impressively sharp as determined by feeling with a thumb or finger.

If desired, the sandstone pebble may also be used to smooth the entire body of the axehead. This adds nothing functionally, but the short time required to smooth and polish the finished tool can be richly rewarding aesthetically. Some stoneworkers go so far as to smooth out the hafting groove, even though the groove is not visible when the axe is secured in its handle. Be careful here — too much polishing has its drawbacks. It is possible to become enthralled with a finely made implement and then not want to put it to practical use.

PHOTO #16: The author demonstrates correct technique for getting
    started on a typical stone mortar.

IMPLEMENTS OF FOOD PREPARATION

The traditional implements of food preparation are the mortar/pestle and metate/mano. The former is a stone bowl (mortar) and hand tool (pestle) used to crush or pound nuts and seeds, while the latter is a flat slab (metate) and a different hand tool (mano) used to grind similar foodstuffs. These implements are made by pecking and grinding, and their manufacture varies only slightly from the techniques used to fabricate hammers and axes.

Mortars can be manufactured from just about any size or shape of coarse-grained rock. I have made several mortars from squarish blocks of stone, but for aesthetic reasons I prefer to use well-rounded stream cobbles. These should be homogeneous and must

PHOTO #17: The final step in manufacturing a stone mortar is abrading the bowl with a sandstone pebble.

be of coarse stone (or they will take seemingly for-ever to manufacture). The bowl is pecked out using the techniques discussed previously. The only varia-tion is that the large size of most mortars makes it difficult to support them on a log or tree stump. I thus prefer to support the mortar stone directly on firm ground. A large mortar will obviously take considerable time to shape, but a small one (such as the one shown in Photograph #17) should only take five or six hours.

Once the bowl has been pecked into shape, it should be ground smooth before use. If you don't smooth it out, you will have increased likelihood of ending up with rock "grit" in your foodstuffs. To smooth the bowl, fill it with water and vigorously abrade it with a sandstone pebble. This grinding should take only a few minutes, and it is a fitting last touch to any mortar.

A pestle can be pecked into shape from a hand-sized piece of coarse stone (such as granite). It's much easier, however, to look for a piece of stone which can be used "as is". I typically use small stream cobbles which are elliptical or cylindrical and which have been worn very smooth. All in all, you should be able to manufacture a usable mortar/pestle set in well under ten hours (though this does not in-clude time spent searching for the right materials).

Instead of or in addition to a mortar/pestle set, you might like to make a metate/mano combina-tion. Rather than make a metate, it is better to locate a sufficiently flat piece of stone. I've found that sandstone slabs make ideal metates, and typically, no alteration is required. The mano, on the other hand, will probably require some work. Select a small flat stone that comfortably fits your hand. Unless one side is already perfectly flat, you will need to grind it down. Using the same tech-niques and materials discussed previously under axe-grinding, you should be able to quickly work your mano into shape. The only thing left is to gather some nuts or seeds and put your new tools to work.

PHOTO #18: A finished metate and mano shown after being used to grind seeds.

CONCLUSION

A concluding word on the manufacturer of stone tools: A friend once remarked that he considered chopping firewood to be highly therapeutic work.   I concur wholeheartedly, and would like to add my own comment.   Not only is chopping wood rewarding, but the hours spent making the axe can be equally relaxing and rewarding.   It all depends on mental attitude.   When I settle down to a long pecking or grinding session, I try to work at a steady, rhythmic pace.   The effect is much the same as chanting or meditating.

Many stoneworkers shy away from pecked and ground stone technology because the work is too tedious.   But it need not be.   If you would like to make a hammer or axe, try to think of your efforts as recreation — not labor.   Also, don't be overly ambitious in the beginning.   Start by making a simple hammer or food muller out of coarse granite.   The work will be rewarding in the sense that progress is readily apparent. But if you start on a fine-grained axe blank, progress will be slow and discouraging. Give this stoneworking technology a proper chance, and you're likely to find it richly rewarding.

PHOTO #19: Rawhide strips were used to haft this basalt axe head
to a willow handle. (Note: this is the same axe head seen
previously in Photo #11, Chapter VI.)

CHAPTER VII

HAFTING TECHNIQUES

In order to put your newly-made stone tools to practical use, they must first be hafted. That is, arrowheads need to be attached to arrow shafts, knife blades should be placed on handles, and axes, hammers, and celts must also be equipped with handles. If your sole interest is making flintknapped artifacts for display, then you will not need the information presented here. But if you would like to put your tools to work, you will need to become familiar with the following guidelines on hafting techniques.

WILLOW

To begin with, we need to be able to identify willow — a common shrub/tree whose wood is useful in all aspects of hafting. Willow can be used for bows, arrows, axe and knife handles, and so forth. It grows in wet ground (typically along streams) throughout the United States. It can grow as a woody shrub or as a tree, and it can be identified by its simple, narrow leaves and slender, smooth-barked twigs.

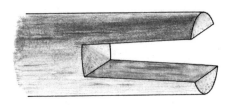

DRAWING #19: Cut a deep and tapering notch in the tip of the arrow shaft.

NOTCHING

Arrow shafts should be provided with notches in order to properly seat the arrowpoint. Notches may be cut with a pocket knife or a sharp-edged stone flake. Since most arrowheads are thicker near the middle than at the base, the notch should be correspondingly tapered (as seen in Drawing #19).

NOTE: the following sections deal only with attaching arrowheads to shafts, not with the construction of the arrow itself. To learn how to make bows, arrows, and related implements, refer to Larry Dean Olsen's book, Outdoor Survival Skills.

SINEW

The classic method for attaching arrowheads to shafts is through use of the sinew-wrap. Sinew is made from the long tendons found on the legs and backs of large animals (deer, cow, etc.). Most butcher shops will be able to provide you with these tendons — typically free for the asking.

To prepare sinew for hafting, the first step is to scrape off any muscle tissue or fat which might be clinging to the tendons. Then rinse the tendons clean and place them in the sun to dry until hard. From this point, the sinew can be processed in one of two ways. The simplest (if you're not squeamish) is to tear off thin sections of dried sinew, place them in your mouth, and chew them for a few minutes. Once the sinew has been chewed to a pulpy texture, tear off individual strands and immediately use these to wrap the arrowhead (as shown in Photograph #20). The sinew does not need to be tied — it has a gluey texture and will hold itself in place.

The second method for processing sinew is only slightly more involved. Take dried sections of tendon and gently pound them between two smooth rocks. Continue pounding until the sinew becomes stringy, fluffly, and white. At this point, tear off individual strands, soak them in water, and proceed as above. The only drawback to using sinew is that it

PHOTO #20: Sinew is commonly utilized to haft arrowpoints to
their shafts.

holds only as long as it remains dry. Should your arrows be exposed to moisture, your sinew-wrap will start to unravel. To prevent this, use a dab of pine pitch to make a watertight seal over the sinew (see next section).

PINE PITCH

Pine pitch may be used as a glue to attach arrowpoints to shafts; also, a thin layer can be used to form a watertight seal over sinew. To gather pitch, search for scarred pine trees which have oozed large quantities of sap (pitch). Once you have obtained a sufficient supply, the pitch can be processed in two different ways. The simplest is to boil the pitch for 3 — 5 minutes. Do not boil any longer; if you do, the pitch will dry hard and brittle and will be of limited use. Also, be careful: pitch is highly flammable.

The second processing method is a little more involved, but it yields a better quality glue. Using two smooth rocks, grind some hardwood charcoal into powder. Then add a small quantity of powdered charcoal to melted (not boiled) pitch. Regardless of how your pitch is processed, apply it while still hot. Dab some into the notch, position the point, and then carefully spread a little more around the point's base. To finish, smooth with your fingers after the pitch has cooled a bit — but before it has completely set. When the pitch has set, it will hold the point securely in place.

ASPHALTUM

If you have trouble locating either pitch or sinew, you can use asphaltum as a binding agent. Historically, asphaltum is an authentic means of hafting — it was the preferred means of the Chumash and other tribes. It can be found naturally at tar pits and oozes, or it can be obtained commercially (roofing asphalt).

Take a small chunk of asphalt, and melt it in an old pot or can. Then apply in the same manner as described above for pine pitch.

PHOTO #21: Three samples of stone knives made by the author.
    LEFT: Antler handle (refer to drawing #20, this chapter).
    MIDDLE: Pine pitch haft
    RIGHT: Backed-blade knife

WOOD or BONE-HANDLED KNIFE

Pine pitch or asphaltum can be used to attach knife blades to wood or bone handles — much in the same manner that these substances were used to haft arrowheads. A good knife handle can be made from a piece of willow about 6" long and 1" diameter (or an equivalently-sized piece of bone). The handle should be notched about 1" deep, and this notch should provide a snug fit for the knife blade. Process the pitch as outlined above and use generous quantities to haft the knife (also as described above).

ANTLER HANDLE KNIFE

A highly functional and aesthetically pleasing knife handle can be made from a short piece of deer or elk antler. To use this hafting technique, you will need a knife blade with a pronounced tang (see Drawing #20). The hafting process is very simple — just boil the antler until the interior is mushy (this should take about half an hour). Then support the knife blade on a wood anvil and carefully drive on the antler handle.

BACKED-BLADE KNIFE

A backed-blade knife is a specialized tool useful for cutting leather, meat, plants, and other soft materials. To make one, you will need a long, thin blade with a straight, feather edge. If you do not have a suitable blade, you can still make this knife by using several shorter pieces. The blade must be "backed"; that is, the non-cutting edge should be dulled — use your pressure flaking tool to do this.

A long, slender piece of willow (about 8"x1/2") will make a good handle. Using a knife or burin (see Chapter VI), score a long deep notch on the handle. Then use hot pine pitch to glue the dulled side of the blade into this notch.

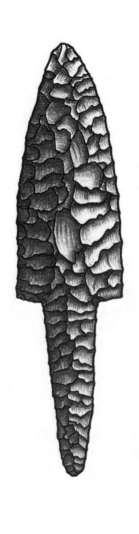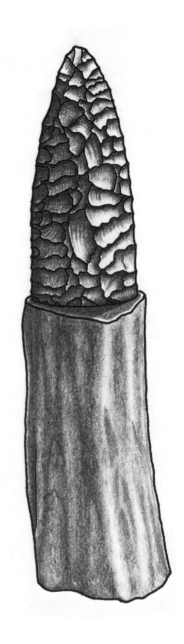

DRAWING #20: Only knife blades with well-pronounced tangs
are suitable for driving into antler handles.

RAWHIDE-WRAPPED AXE

When rawhide is soaked in water, it becomes soft
and pliable. But as it dries, it shrinks slightly
and becomes very stiff. Because of these characteristics, rawhide strips are ideal for hafting axes and
hammers (see photograph at the start of this chapter).
The manufacture of rawhide is an involved process
that takes several days. If you would like to make
your own, you will find complete directions in the
book Outdoor Survival Skills by Larry Olsen. It
should be possible, however, to secure a supply of
ready-to-use rawhide.

Many leather-supply houses can provide you with
pieces of rawhide. Other possible sources include
Indian curio shops, a "mountain man" rendezvous, or
your friendly neighborhood survival student. But the
surest source of all is a pet store — small pieces
of rawhide are sold there as "doggie chews".

To haft an axe with rawhide, you will first need
to carve a suitable handle. This can be made from
a willow branch about 12-14" long and 1½-2" thick.
Thin the bottom to a comfortable fit for your hand,
but leave the top wide enough to support the axe.
Finally, the top should be carved to perfectly fit
the axe head (this may require a bit of ingenuity).

Soak your rawhide for 12-20 hours, or until
thoroughly pliable. Then cut it into a long strip
about 1/4" wide. If you are using small pieces of
rawhide (the "doggie chews"), you will probably only
be able to get about three feet of thong from each
piece — in which case you will need several. While
the rawhide is still wet and pliable, use it to secure the axehead in place. Be sure to stretch the
rawhide tight and tie off securely. Finally, allow
the rawhide to dry slowly and thoroughly. It will
dry very hard and will grip the axehead firmly.

A final comment on rawhide: it has the same
disadvantage as sinew; that is, it will not hold when
wet. Therefore, to finish your rawhide-wrapped axe,
brush a light coating of hot pine pitch over the rawhide thongs.

SEQUENCE OF PHOTOS SHOWING HOW TO WRAP A WILLOW HANDLE ONTO AN AXE HEAD. (Note: this is the same axe previously seen in photos 12-15, Chapter VI).

PHOTO #22: Wrapping the willow onto the axe head. The most common error is to use willow too thick for the purpose. Note that this willow is of a thickness equal to that of the little finger.

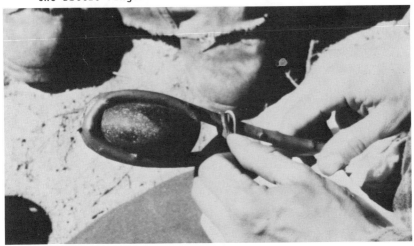

PHOTO #23: Securing the willow-wrap handle with a leather thong.

PHOTO #24: The finished axe — ready for use.

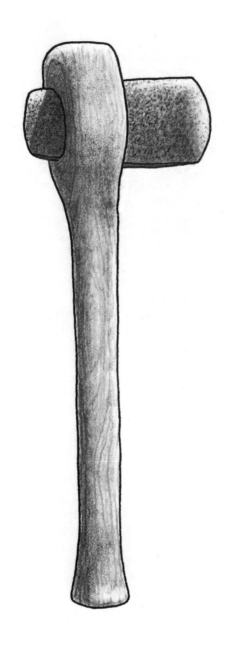

DRAWING #21: Artist's depiction of a typical stone celt
    and handle.

WILLOW-WRAP AXE

A small stone hammer or axe can be quickly and easily hafted with willow. For the willow-wrap handle, a slender willow is selected and heated over the coals of a fire. The willow should be slowly twirled in order to assure uniform heating. When steam is heard escaping, the willow is ready for use. It is now pliable and can be easily wrapped around the hammer or axehead. Hold the axe near the center of the willow and wrap each end completely around the stone. Then quickly secure the willow with leather thongs, rawhide, or any other available cordage. If no cord is available, the haft may be secured with young willow shoots, but these too should first be made more pliable by heating over coals.

The willow-wrap handle looks delicate and does not inspire great confidence. In order to satisfy my curiosity, I determined to find the haft's breaking point. I accordingly took the small hand axe pictured here, and attempted to break it. I started chopping on a fallen oak tree, using both hands and all my strength. Both a friend and I tried for some time, but we were not able to break the handle. When we finally quit, we were both highly impressed by the strength of this "delicate" handle.

CELT

The celt is a specialized form of axe. The celt stone is made in a wedge-shape, and does not have hafting grooves. It is made thinner and narrower at the butt than at the chopping edge. It is then slipped into a corresponding hole which is carved completely through a handle. The completed celt is the essence of simplicity and ruggedness — the more it is used, the tighter the head is wedged in place.

An average celt handle can be whittled from a willow branch 2-2½" diameter by about 18" in length. The bottom is trimmed to a comfortable fit for the hand, but the top should be left large and bulky to provide support for the celt stone.

USING STONE TOOLS

Now that you have hafted your stone tools, you are ready to put them to practical use. A backed-blade knife is sharper than surgical steel, and it will cut leather and other soft materials with amazing efficiency. The more traditional wood or antler-handled knife will make a useful general purpose tool. However, it does have a few drawbacks. It will not readily slice through wood — to cut a branch, use a sawing rather than a slicing motion. Also, it will have limited value as a wood-shaver (a sharp square-edged flake works better). Your knife will dull during use and will need to be resharpened. To do this, use your pressure flaking tool to snap off tiny pieces up and down both edges (but from only one side).

A stone hammer can be put to a variety of practical uses — use it to pound jerky for pemmican, to separate fibers from plants (for making cordage), to break the grain of rawhide, etc. For information on these and related skills, once again refer to Olsen's book, Outdoor Survival Skills.

A properly-made stone axe or celt will make a very practical chopping tool. It will probably impress you with its efficiency, though admittedly, modern steel axes are more effective. The stone axe can be used to chop firewood, cut down trees, etc. Small trees (up to 4" diameter) can be cut in a matter of minutes; larger trees will take considerably longer. The random cutting of trees cannot be condoned, but if a genuine need exists, a good stone axe will do the work.

Once you have a good set of prehistoric tools (bow, arrows, knife, hammer and axe), all you'll need are moccasins and a loin cloth to take up an aboriginal life style. Using these tools, you can make a fire-bow set, prepare shelters, hunt and dress game, and so forth. To be honest, I don't seriously expect anyone to return to the stone age; my point is that these tools can provide for all human needs — as indeed they did for countless ages.

PHOTO #25: Don Fisher is shown knapping at a typical backyard waste collection pit.

CHAPTER VIII

ETHICS

Modern knappers have the potential to make significant contributions to the archaeologist's knowledge of aboriginal stone working techniques. The reverse, unfortunately, is equally possible. If contemporary workers are not conscientious, their activities can be seriously disruptive. Archaeological sites can be destroyed, new sites can be inadvertently created, and newly-made replicas can be mistaken for original specimens. All of these problems can be avoided by adhering to the following simple guidelines.

SITE PRESERVATION

Perhaps the greatest abuse of inexperienced knappers is the disturbance of aboriginal sites. All too frequently, beginners gather their lithic materials in the form of waste chips and flakes left behind by prehistoric craftsmen. This practice cannot be condoned. Waste lithic material (properly known as debitage) is of great value to the archaeologist.

Finished artifacts show the scars of only the last flakes removed by the craftsman. Scientists thus need the total debitage to ascertain the entire manufacturing sequence. Even if no finished artifacts are available, the debitage alone tells what was being manufactured. Debitage is thus scientifically important, and it should not be disturbed. No matter how difficult it may be to find workable stone, never despoil the archaeological record by gathering flakes left behind by native craftsmen. Remember, if absolutely no other lithic material is available, one can always begin with window, stained, or bottle glass.

Experienced knappers prefer to manufacture their own flakes, and thus are not interested in picking up waste flakes and chips. Their concern is to find usable cobbles and nodules, not debitage. But they too have to be careful. Much lithic material is today gathered from sources which were once aboriginal quarries. Even if nodules alone are gathered, it is still possible to disrupt the record of prehistoric activities. The solution, for the conscientious artisan, is to collect material only from areas that are already grossly disturbed. In other words, material should be gathered from road cuts, construction zones, and other similarly damaged localities.

DEBITAGE DISPOSAL

Another concern to the modern knapper is that the debitage created today not be mistaken for a prehistoric site tomorrow (tomorrow, of course, might be a hundred years away). If knapping is done indoors, disposal of debitage is easy: simply throw it out with the trash. It is hard to imagine a city dump being mistaken for anything else. But if knapping is done outdoors (even in the backyard), then proper disposal is a necessity. Your backyard may seem a far cry from a prehistoric archaeological site, but one cannot be certain that circumstances will never change. At some unforeseen future date, new construction might expose the results of backyard knapping activities. And if you are not around a few centuries hence, who will explain what took place?

To properly dispose of outdoor debitage, dig a waste pit beforehand. By working at the edge of the pit, it should be quite easy to keep waste material confined to it. Once knapping activities cease, whether it be later the same day or years hence, the pit should be covered. Before filling, however, be sure to mix in items which would date your activity. A few coins would be best, but some recent charcoal (for radiocarbon dating) could be added for further protection.

If your outdoor knapping activities are to be quite brief, you may not wish to go to the trouble of digging a pit. In this case, simply spread out a sturdy groundcloth before beginning. Be careful about your knapping and keep debitage confined to the ground cover. By so doing, you will be able to easily remove your debitage and take it elsewhere for proper disposal.

SIGNING REPLICAS

When modern craftsmen duplicate prehistoric points using authentic techniques and materials, it can sometimes be difficult distinguishing the replica from the original. This is particularly true if the knapper is dishonest, and attempts to pass his work

PHOTO #26: Don Fisher demonstrates use of a small electric engraver of the type capable of engraving flintknapped artifacts.

as authentic prehistoric artifacts. Most knappers, of course, would never intentionally misrepresent their work. The problem arises later, after artifacts have changed hands. No matter how honest the knapper, there is always the chance that someone will mistake new work for authentic specimens. The only solution is for the knapper to sign his or her replications.

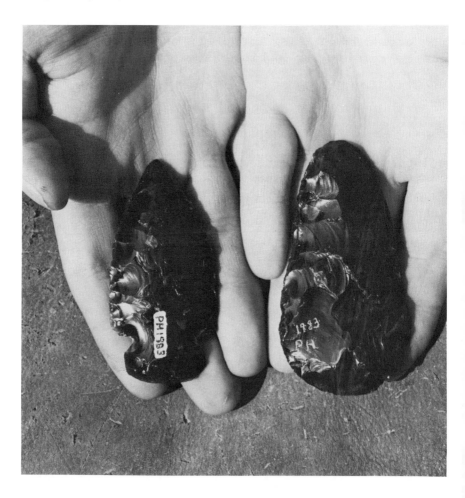

PHOTO #27: Two artifacts signed and dated by the author.
   LEFT: Pen and ink
   RIGHT: Engraved

A permanent mark can be made on replicas with a small, hand-held electric engraver. Such engravers are commonly used to mark valuables, and they are thus readily available. They are amazingly efficient and will easily engrave even the hardest lithic materials. One can be used to engrave either the knapper's initials, the date, or some other identifying mark on newly-made artifacts.

If engraving is not your style, then you can sign your replications with pen and ink. If the lithic material is light-colored, then sign it directly with a permanent black ink. But if using obsidian or other dark material, it will first be necessary to brush on a contrasting patch of white ink in order for your mark to be readily visible. Even if artifacts never leave your possession, they should still be signed and dated. For — unless they are buried with you — the day will eventually come when no one will be left to explain their origin.

CONCLUSION

The intent of this chapter has been to alert knappers to potential problems, and not to discourage resourcefulness. The important issue is that contemporary flintknappers help, not hinder, the cause of scientific archaeology. Regardless of your motives for making stone tools, the taking of a few simple precautions will in no way whatsoever lessen your enjoyment. If you're both safety-conscious and mindful of the concerns of professional archaeologists, then your sojourn into stone-working technology should be trouble-free and personally rewarding. For some of us, a lifetime of pleasure and delight is waiting in the form of unworked flint and obsidian nodules. The only way to know what's in store for you is to give it a try.

Have fun, but please do be careful.

APPENDIX I

GLOSSARY

An asterisk (*) denotes terms which are not discussed elsewhere in this book. They have been included here because they are important terms which should be understood by anyone desiring to pursue further knowledge of flintknapping.

ALTERNATE FLAKING: the removal of flakes from alternate sides of the same edge.

BACKED: the intentional dulling of one edge of a flake or blade.

BIFACE: an artifact which has been flaked on both sides.

BILLET: a cylindrical percussor of material other than stone (typically refers to antler percussors).

BLADE: a specialized flake which is more than twice as long as it is wide.

BLANK: a piece of lithic raw material suitable for the making of an artifact.

BURIN: a chisel-like lithic tool.

CELT: a specialized wedge-shaped form of axe.

CONCHOIDAL FRACTURE: a fracture in which the radiating fracture lines take on a cone-like appearance.

CORE: a mass of lithic material from which flakes are struck; frequently preshaped to a desired form for the removal of specific flakes or blades.

CORTEX: the outer rind or skin of a piece of lithic material.

CRYPTOCRYSTALLINE: a crystal structure so fine-grained that the crystals cannot be seen.

DEBITAGE: waste lithic material.

DISTAL (*): the "bottom" of a flake or blade; that is, the edge farthest away from the striking platform.

DORSAL (*):   the "back" of a flake or blade; that is, the side
        away from the rock core (from which the flake was struck).

ELASTIC: a property of stone that returns to its original form
        after being compressed by the application of a force.

END SHOCK: a fracture which runs straight and has a slightly
        lipped edge.

FEATHER FRACTURE: the ideal fracture; that is, one that termi-
        nates in a feather-thin edge.

FLAKING: the process of removing small pieces (flakes) from a
        lithic core by either percussion or pressure.

FLINT: a highly siliceous mineral which is ideal for knapping.

FLINTKNAPPING: to break flint with a sharp blow; that is, the
        manufacture of percussion or pressure flaked artifacts.

FLUTE: a large longitudinal flake scar on a projectile point.

GRINDING: the wearing away of lithic material by abrasion.

HAMMERSTONE: a hand-held stone used as a percussor or pecking
        agent.

HEAT TREATMENT: the thermal alteration of stone to improve its
        flaking characteristics.

HINGE FRACTURE: a fracture that terminates a flake or blade with
        a round or blunt break.

HOMOGENEOUS: lithic material of the same structure throughout.

INCLUSION: a foreign body or impurity in a piece of lithic
        material.

INDIRECT PERCUSSION: percussion flaking in which an intermediate
        tool is used to transfer the force of the percussor.

ISOTROPIC: lithic material which has the same properties in all
        directions.

LITHIC: anything pertaining to stone (derived from the Greek
        "lithos", which means "stone").

MANO: a hand-held food grinding implement.

METATE: a flat slab of stone used for grinding foodstuffs with a
        mano.

MORTAR: a stone bowl used for the pounding or crushing of food-stuffs (used with a pestle).

OBSIDIAN: volcanic stone which is the natural equivalent of glass.

PECKING: the removal of minute quantities of material by crushing or crumbling through repeated hammerstone blows.

PERCUSSION FLAKING: the dynamic striking of flakes from a lithic core.

PERVERSE FRACTURE: a spiral or twisting fracture which typically does not run straight.

PESTLE: a hand-held food crushing implement (used with a mortar).

PLATFORM: surface on which the flake-detaching force is applied.

PREFORM (*): the unfinished stage in the manufacture of an arti-fact (after the artifact has undergone initial shaping).

PRESSURE FLAKING: the static pressing away of small pieces of lithic material.

PROXIMAL (*): the "top" of a flake or blade; that is, the edge nearest the striking platform.

PUNCH: the intermediate tool employed during indirect percussion (typically made of antler).

SILICEOUS: a silica bearing lithic material; that is, material suited for flintknapping.

SPALL: a small fragment or chip of lithic material.

STEP FRACTURE: a fracture that terminates a flake or blade abruptly with a right angle break.

TANG: a projecting shank used to attach a tool to its handle.

TINE: the slender pointed tip of an antler.

TRUNCATE: to shorten by cutting off an end.

UNIFACE (*): an artifact which as been flaked on only one side.

VENTRAL (*): the "front" of a flake or blade; that is, the side facing the rock core (from which the flake was struck).

VITREOUS: lithic material having the near texture and luster of glass.

APPENDIX II

RECOMMENDED READING

The major references utilized in the preparation of this book are listed below. All are valuable reference works, and they are recommended for anyone desiring to further pursue the study of flintknapping. Addresses for ordering have been included. Since prices are subject to change, they have not been listed here. Please inquire about price and availability before ordering.

Callahan, Errett. The Basics of Biface Knapping in the Eastern Fluted Point Tradition: A Manual for Flintknappers and Lithic Analysts, V. 7, Archaeology of Eastern North America, Eastern States Archeological Federation, Connecticut, 1979.

A detailed and valuable scientific reference for all knappers. Highly recommended. Order from:

Eastern States Archeological Federation
American Indian Archaeological Institute
Washington, Connecticut 06793

Crabtree, Don E. Experiments in Flintworking. Idaho State University Museum, 1971.

Crabtree, Don E. An Introduction to Flintworking, Occasional Paper #28, Idaho State University Museum, 1972.

These two works by Crabtree are the "bibles" of modern flintknapping. Excellent information on terminology, scientific principles, etc. A must for serious students of flintknapping. Order from:

Idaho State University Museum
Campus Box 8096
Idaho State University
Pocatello, Idaho   83209

Jamison, Richard L.   The Best of Woodsmoke.
    Horizon, 1982.

    A highly useful book for anyone desiring to
    round out their knowledge of wilderness survival
    and aboriginal living techniques.   Includes in-
    formation on primitive fire-making, shelters,
    etc.   Order from:

        WOODSMOKE JOURNAL
        P. O. Box 474
        Centerville, Utah   84014

Olsen, Larry Dean.   Outdoor Survival Skills.   Brigham
    Young University Press, 1973.

    A valuable reference on skills related to flint-
    knapping — processing sinew and rawhide, etc.
    Available at bookstores or order from the
    publisher:

        Brigham Young University Press
        218 University Building
        Provo, Utah   84602

Waldorf, D.C.   The Art of Flint Knapping.   Mound
    Builder Books, 1979.

    A useful reference for anyone desiring to see a
    second perspective on the "how to" of stone
    tool-making.   Order from:

        Mound Builder Books
        D. C. Waldorf
        P. O. Box 702
        Branson, Missouri 65616

APPENDIX III

SUPPLY SOURCE

Tips have been provided throughout the text to help the beginner procure the tools necessary for flintknapping — antler and copper pressure flakers, hammerstones, billets, and so forth. If difficulty is encountered obtaining these supplies, then they can be purchased from the following source.

PILTDOWN PRODUCTIONS — Directed by Dr. Errett Callahan.
Specializes in state-of-the-art obsidian knives. Also provides a range of tools, instructional materials, and workshops for the amateur and advanced flintknapper. For current catalog, send $5.00 to:

> PILTDOWN PRODUCTIONS
> 2 Fredonia Avenue
> Lynchburg, VA 24503